stash happy FELT

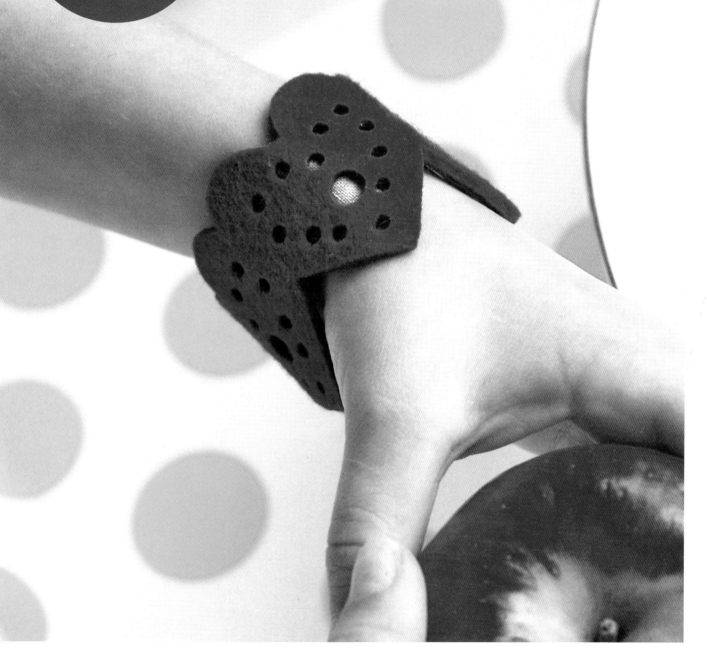

stash happy

FELT

30 FUN PROJECTS FOR FELT (AND FABRIC) LOVERS

Amanda Carestio

LARK CRAFTS

An Imprint of Sterling Publishing Co., Inc.
New York

WWW.LARKCRAFTS.COM

ASSISTANT EDITOR: *Thom O'Hearn*

ART DIRECTOR: *Megan Kirby*

DESIGNER: *Julie Tietsort*

ILLUSTRATOR: *Orrin Lungdren*

PHOTOGRAPHER: *Cynthia Shaffer*

COVER DESIGNER: *Pamela Norman*

Library of Congress Cataloging-in-Publication Data

Carestio, Amanda.
  Stash happy : felt : 30 fun projects for felt (and fabric) lovers / Amanda Carestio. -- 1st ed.
     p. cm.
  Includes index.
  ISBN 978-1-60059-925-5
  1. ˇFelt work. ˇI. Title.
ˇˇTT849.5.C384 2011
ˇˇ746'.0463--dc22
                                               2010053998
 10 9 8 7 6 5 4 3 2 1

First Edition

Published by Lark Crafts
An Imprint of Sterling Publishing Co., Inc.
387 Park Avenue South, New York, NY 10016

© 2011, Lark Crafts, an Imprint of Sterling Publishing Co., Inc.

Distributed in Canada by Sterling Publishing,
c/o Canadian Manda Group, 165 Dufferin Street
Toronto, Ontario, Canada M6K 3H6

Distributed in the United Kingdom by GMC Distribution Services,
Castle Place, 166 High Street, Lewes, East Sussex, England BN7 1XU

Distributed in Australia by Capricorn Link (Australia) Pty Ltd.,
P.O. Box 704, Windsor, NSW 2756 Australia

If you have questions or comments about this book, please contact:
Lark Crafts
67 Broadway
Asheville, NC 28801
828-253-0467

Manufactured in China

ISBN 13: 978-1-60059-925-5

For information about custom editions, special sales, premium and corporate purchases, please contact Sterling Special Sales Department at 800-805-5489 or specialsales@sterlingpub.com.

For information about desk and examination copies available to college and university professors, requests must be submitted to academic@larkbooks.com. Our complete policy can be found at www.larkcrafts.com.

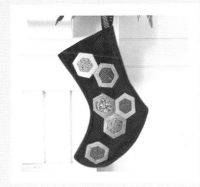

page 19

page 25

page 86

page 40

stash happy FELT

online!

Find a handful of
free bonus projects at
www.larkcrafts.com/bonus.

Never felt better!

If you're anything like me, you thought accumulating fabric was the easiest thing in the world. Then you started buying felt!

It began with those notebook-sized sheets. They're so cheap, it's hard not to buy a few every time you're at the craft store! Then you were captivated by a bigger project and bought some felt off those 54-inch bolts. Well, if they're cutting it anyways, might as well buy a few extra inches...And then one day you figured out how to felt wool sweaters. Thrift stores never looked the same again.

No matter how you were ensnared, or how much felt is in your stash, there's lots to adore about this lovely, fuzzy stuff. It's tough, it doesn't ravel, and it's perfect for appliqué and cozies of all kinds.

This book explores a variety of projects to put your extra inches and yards to good use. Whether you want to feature a favorite color, showcase a former sweater, or just play with bits and pieces, there are enough designs to keep you busy. Want to add other fabrics to the mix? Glad you asked! Felt plays so well with other cotton prints, linen, repurposed fabrics—the more, the merrier!

All 30 designs are creative, captivating, and ready for you to make them your own.

- Keep the scraps in the sewing room, but make them work a little harder! Whip up the Sewing Machine Cozy (page 90) or Whale Pincushion (page 52) to decorate your space.
- Stuffed friends like the Woodland Bear (page 110) and Owl Plush Toy (page 56) are cozier to cuddle when they're made of felt!
- Take a break with a wee bit of needle felting. The Mushroom Terrarium (page 60) elevates earthy-colored roving.
- Felt is also the perfect canvas for embroidery. You can see for yourself when you sew the Gift Tags (page 102) or Felt-Framed Portraits (page 82).

Even if you don't have much time, skim through these pages and find a fast one, maybe something of the no-sew variety. Perfect for adding a little touch of creativity to your day... or for sneaking in some craft time while a little one eats, sleeps, or is otherwise distracted.

Have fun with your felt stash...and get stash happy!

basics

gather

The hardest thing about "gathering" is trying to avoid it, especially when it comes to felt and fabric goodies! These projects are designed to make the most of what you already have, but we won't tell.

Felt, Fabulous Felt!

So I'll admit it: I'm a little crazy for felt. It's just lovely stuff! Between those super-wide bolts and those inexpensive so-buy-one-in-every-color sheets, felt stash pretty much gathers itself. And these days, crafters have lots of options, especially if you're willing to shop online.

The projects in this book use the following types of felt:

- Acrylic and wool felt
- Recycled sweater felt (see page 10)
- Eco and bamboo felt
- Industrial felt (strong, thick stuff!)
- Adhesive felt
- Prefelt sheets and wool roving (for needle felting)

And don't forget the fabric! We had lots of fun pairing fabric and felt in these projects; there's something extra special about this combination of textures. You'll need several other odds and ends, too. Some projects will call for stuffing, buttons, ribbons, embroidery floss, elastic, cording, piping, grommets and setter, and various clasps.

basic felt sewing kit

- ★ Sewing machine
- ★ Rotary cutter and mat
- ★ Ruler
- ★ Scissors
- ★ Straight pins
- ★ Iron and pressing cloth
- ★ Basting spray, fabric glue, or fusible web
- ★ Hand-sewing and embroidery needles
- ★ Disappearing ink fabric marker
- ★ Pinking shears (optional)

make

Once you've taken proper stock of your stash, you're ready to get to work. Here are a few tips and techniques for working with felt.

Using Templates

All the templates you'll need are in the back of the book, starting on page 114. Use the enlargement percentages listed as a guide or use your own calculations, based on how big you want your finished project to be. If you've never worked with felt before, you'll realize soon enough that is has a tendency to be a bit shifty. My favorite technique for using templates—especially small shapes—is to cut out the paper template, trace that shape onto the felt with a disappearing ink fabric marker, and then cut along the lines.

> **TIP**
> If you're working with two layers, trace around your paper template shape with a marker, stitch along the drawn line, and then cut around the outside edge of the stitched line.

For the larger shapes, I'll usually pin and then cut out around the edges of the shape, either with sharp scissors or a rotary cutter.

Cut It Out!

There's nothing too mysterious about cutting felt, other than the fact that you'll need sharp scissors or a sharp rotary blade to get a clean edge. Pinking shears and felt also make a lovely combination! For teeny tiny shapes, you could also consider using a craft paper punch or a die cut; you'll probably want to experiment a little first.

Stitch It Good!

Again, nothing too difficult about sewing with felt, but there are a few tricks that can make your life easier—especially when you're working with scraps and with a thick material like felt.

Some of these projects involve stitching through *many* layers of both felt and fabric. It's probably breaking some sacred rule, but I often use my sewing machine's walking foot when working with felt. This particular foot can help make sure those layers travel through the machine at the same speed, though it can create a little fuzz on your top layer of felt—I just trim this off with sharp scissors. For those extra thick areas, you might also try a lighter pressure on your presser foot.

Don't have the exact size scrap you need? It's easy to join two felt shapes together: Simply run them side-by-side through your sewing machine and use a relatively wide zigzag stitch to join the two pieces together.

Appliqué Away

Appliqué is one of my favorite techniques to use with felt, whether I'm stitching with my sewing machine or by hand. The techniques are pretty much the same as with other types of fabric, but it's actually a bit easier with felt than, say, cotton, since you don't have to worry about raveling edges (see Dealing with Edges on page 11). And felt is a perfect fit, in my humble opinion, for reverse appliqué.

If you're machine appliquéing felt shapes, keep in mind that felt tends to squirm a bit under the presser foot, so you'll need to do something to keep it in place while you stitch. A handy trick for this step is to use basting spray (sometimes in combination with pins). You could also use fabric glue or even fusible web, though you'll want to use a pressing cloth when ironing felt and you'll probably want to test a sample first, just to make sure you don't end up with a big melty mess.

If you're hand-stitching your shapes in place, you might have an easier time controlling the felt. You've got options when it comes to stitches to use: blanket stitch, whipstitch, and a simple running stitch (all on page 9) are all quite useful and easy to create.

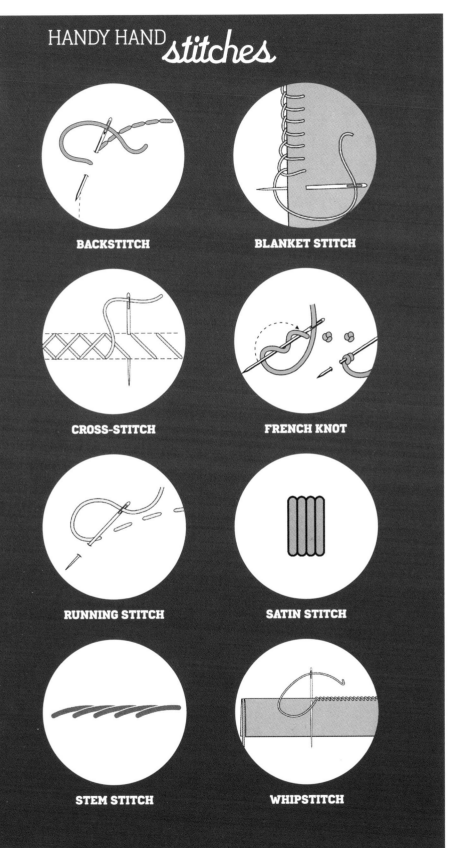

HANDY HAND *stitches*

BACKSTITCH

BLANKET STITCH

CROSS-STITCH

FRENCH KNOT

RUNNING STITCH

SATIN STITCH

STEM STITCH

WHIPSTITCH

Embroidery

Whether it's a useful blanket stitch or a prim and pretty French knot, I love combining felt and embroidery stitches. For transferring patterns, a disappearing fabric marker is your new best friend. And try using more strands of your floss (maybe four strands instead of two) to make sure your stitches really show up against the felt background. Here's a handy chart (at left) with all the stitches you'll need for the projects in this book.

needle felting

Sewing felt is the main focus of the projects in this book, but a few needle-felting basics will serve you well when you decide you can't live without a project like Lisa Jordan's Mushroom Terrarium (page 60). The project instructions will tell you everything you need to know.

No-Sew Projects

In the midst of a last-minute gift snafu? We've got you covered. Several of the projects in this book come together without a single stitch. For these, you'll need some kind of glue product such as fabric glue or a hot glue gun. Make a lovely wreath (page 32), a too-cute set of felt trees (page 78), or a darling Heart Bracelet (page 64; okay, not technically no-sew but pretty darn close!).

how to felt a sweater

Mary Rasch provided these handy instructions for turning an old sweater into your new favorite felt fabric; see her projects on pages 66 and 88.

❶ Begin by selecting a sweater that is 100% wool. You can also try natural fibers such as mohair, lambswool, or angora, but each will create a different feel in the finished product. If you are making a project for a baby or young child, consider using the least scratchy fiber possible, such as lambswool or angora.

❷ Stuff your sweater into a laundry bag and place it in the washing machine. Fill the machine with a small amount of hot water and a dash of mild soap (such as dish soap, wool wash, or a mild detergent). The felting process needs friction, so toss in tennis balls, dryer balls, or even tennis shoes.

❸ Allow your washer to go through the wash cycle but stop it before the spin cycle, as this cycle can create permanent creases in your sweater. Continually check on the progress of the felting and feel free to repeat the washing process to achieve a more felted look.

❹ Let your sweater air-dry on a flat surface before beginning your project.

DEALING WITH *edges*

Okay, and now for the best part: you don't have to! This simple fact makes up a goodly portion of the reason I love felt so much. No freezer paper, no painstakingly turned edges...unless, of course, you just want to! If not, you've got plenty of options for how to treat your edges:

Leave the edges raw or pinked.

*Blanket-stitch
for a nice clean finish.*

Use felt as binding.

*Whipstitch
over the edge.*

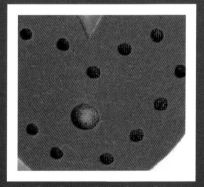

Skip the stitching altogether.

Even more stashy goodness online!

Want even more ideas for how to use your felt stash with flair? Download these free projects at www.LarkCrafts.com/Bonus:

Bauble Bracelets

Fascinator Headband

autumn leaves
COFFEE COZY

Keep the coffee in your French press nice
and warm no matter what the season.

designed by: *laura howard*

from your stash

Piece of beige felt,
9 x 12 inches (22.9 x 30.5 cm)

Piece of dark brown felt,
9 x 12 inches (22.9 x 30.5 cm)

Felt scraps in red, orange,
and mustard yellow

gather

Basic felt sewing kit (page 7)

Templates (page 126)

Beige thread

1 yard (1 m) of narrow trim,
tape, or cord in linen or natural
colored cotton

make

❶ Trace the cozy template from page 126 onto the beige felt as close to the
edge of the felt as possible. Cut out the shape (this will be the front). The
leftover felt will be used in step 5.

❷ Repeat step 1 using the dark brown felt (this will be the back).

❸ Trace the leaf template from page 126 onto the colorful scraps thirty times
and cut out the shapes. Arrange the leaves in rows along the front of the cozy,
so you have 10 rows with three leaves in each row. Make sure the rows are as
straight as possible, with even gaps between them and a random-looking mix
of colors. When you are happy with the arrangement, pin the leaves in place.

❹ Thread a needle with beige thread to match the cozy. Sew a neat line down
the center of each row of leaves, using a backstitch. Remove the pins as you
sew and take care that the leaves stay straight (**fig. A**).

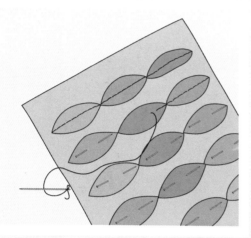

fig. A

fig. B

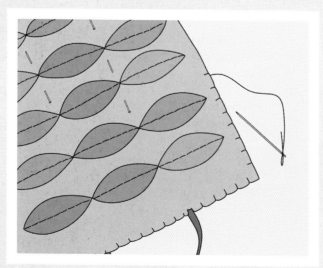

fig. C

❺ Take the leftover felt pieces from step 1 and trim them so they are the same length as the cozy template. Pin the two pieces together along one long edge and sew along the edge using a whipstitch (not too tight!). Remove the pins and press the edge seam open with your fingers so you have one large felt panel (this will become the middle layer of the cozy).

❻ Pin the decorated front cozy piece to the dark brown back piece. Sewing the leaves onto the front may have caused it to shrink slightly in height, and if there has been any shrinkage, trim the dark brown felt to match the front. Trim the middle piece, if needed, so you end up with three rectangles of identical size.

❼ Cut the trim to make four ties, each measuring 10 inches (25.4 cm). Knot each tie at one end to help prevent fraying. Position two of the ties at one end of the middle cozy piece, with the unknotted ends overlapping the felt by about ½ inch (1.3 cm). Sew one in place 1½ inches (3.8 cm) from the top of the cozy and another 1½ inches (3.8 cm) from the bottom, or wherever best suits the position of the handle on your French press **(fig. B)**.

❽ Sandwich your three cozy pieces and pin them together. With the leafy front of your cozy facing towards you, sew all three layers together using light brown thread **(fig. C)**. Use a neat blanket stitch around the edges, with a few extra stitches to help secure the ties. Finish your sewing neatly at the back of the cozy.

variation!

Create a spring-themed cozy with a lighter, greener color palette. Or make a Valentine's Day cozy with rows of cute hearts in red and pink shades.

penny rug BOUQUET

Hand stitching and button centers
give this bunch a little extra punch.

designed by: *lisa jordan*

from your stash

24 circles of felt in assorted
colors and sizes

gather

Basic felt sewing kit (page 7)

6-strand embroidery floss in
assorted colors

Craft knife (optional)

9 feet (2.7 m) of bendable floral
wire (for stems approximately
8 inches [20.3 cm] long)

Wire snippers or pliers

12 small buttons, 6 must be
sew-through

make

a six stem bouquet

1. Gather the felt circles and arrange them into six stacks, with the smallest circle on the top of each stack. You'll need one small, one medium, and two large circles of the same size for each flower.

2. With three strands of embroidery floss, whipstitch the circles together. First stitch the small circle to the medium circle, and then the medium to the large. (You can tack the pieces down with a dot of fabric glue to keep them from moving around while you sew.) With a blanket stitch, attach the stacked circles to another large circle **(fig. A)**.

3. Make a small slit through the center of your stacked circles using the pointed tip of scissors or a craft knife. The slit only needs to be large enough to feed the wire through— and not so large that a button would slip through.

4. Cut a length of floral wire about 18 inches (45.7 cm) long, using your wire snippers. Bend the wire in half, forming an elongated U shape.

5. Choose which button you want to be in the center of your flower, and thread it onto the bent wire.

6. Feed the wire through the slit in the stacked circles until the button sits nicely on the top circle. Thread the second button (a sew-through) onto the wire to sit underneath the bottom of the large circle. This button will keep your stack firmly assembled once the wire is twisted.

fig. A

fig. B

7 Twist the floral wire, holding the buttons and circle stack firmly, until the entire stem has been twisted and the circle stack is secure **(fig. B)**.

8 Snip off any uneven wire ends. You may want to fold or curl the cut ends on themselves so there are no sharp edges.

9 Repeat steps 2 to 8 to make five more flowers.

variation!

Instead of cutting perfect circles, use other organic shapes to make a funky bouquet. You can also use various fabrics and trims instead of felt.

hexy STOCKING

Reverse appliqué hexagons help tiny bits of felt and fabric make a big impact.

designed by: *amanda carestio*

from your stash

2 pieces of red felt, each 12 x 18 inches (30.5 x 45.7 cm)

6 pieces of felt in tan and neutral colors, each 4 x 4 inches (10.2 x 10.2 cm)

6 pieces of red fabric, each 4 x 4 inches (10.2 x 10.2 cm)

Piece of red fabric, 8 inches (20.3 cm) long

gather

Basic felt sewing kit (page 7)

Templates (page 116)

Red and cream thread

Tan piping

fig. A

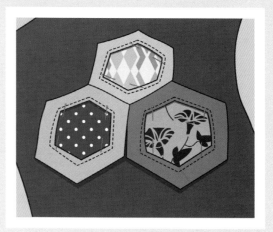

fig. B

make

the hexagons

❶ Enlarge and trace the hexagon template from page 116 onto tan and neutral colored felt scraps six times. Cut out the inside of each shape, leaving a border of about ½ inch (1.3 cm).

❷ Spray baste the back of the hexagon shapes and position them on the red scraps of fabric.

❸ Stitch around the inside edge of the felt borders using cream thread. Trim off the excess fabric, using the felt hexagon shape as a guide **(fig. A)**.

TIP
While you're cutting away the excess fabric, turn the scissors to a 45° angle so the fabric layer is cut slightly smaller than the felt shape.

the stocking

❹ Trace the stocking template from page 116 onto the red felt twice and cut out the shapes. For an exact match, cut the two shapes on folded fabric.

❺ Spray baste the back of the hexagon shapes and position them on the stocking front **(fig. B)**. Pin for added security.

❻ Stitch around the outside edge of each hexagon shape.

the hanging loop

❼ Cut a 1 x 8-inch (2.5 x 20.3 cm) strip from the red felt and a ½ x 8-inch (1.3 x 20.3 cm) strip from the red fabric strip.

❽ Pin and stitch the red fabric strip to the felt strip, leaving the edges raw.

finishing

❾ Pull the cord from the piping and trim the end.

❿ Fold over the end of the piping. Starting from the top right edge of the stocking, pin the piping, wrong sides together, between the front and back of the stocking, inserting the loop at the top right between the front and back stocking layers **(fig. C)**.

⓫ Stitch around the outside edge of the stocking twice with red thread, catching the hanging loop and the piping in the seams.

⓬ When you reach the end of the piping, pull the cord out, trim it, and turn it under as you did in step 10.

variation!

Not hexagon obsessed (yet)? Use a different shape for the reverse appliqué: hearts, stars, and plus signs would all be cute!

fig. C

vintage TRIVET

Colorful, vintage-inspired fabrics
make this doily an instant classic.

designed by: *amanda carestio*

from your stash

2 pieces of felt, each 9 x 12
inches (22.9 x 30.5 cm)

Piece of fabric, 9 x 9 inches
(22.9 x 22.9 cm)

gather

Basic felt sewing kit (page 7)

Template (page 119)

Matching or coordinating thread

Embroidery floss

Bobbin or other small circular
object, to trace

make

❶ Trace the template from page 119 onto one of the pieces of felt and cut
out the shape.

❷ Spray baste the back of the felt shape and position it on top of the fabric.

❸ Stitch around four of the petal shapes with matching or coordinating
sewing thread.

❹ Spray baste the back of the fabric shape and place it on the remaining
piece of felt.

❺ Stitch around the outside edge of the top felt shape, as close to the edge
as possible.

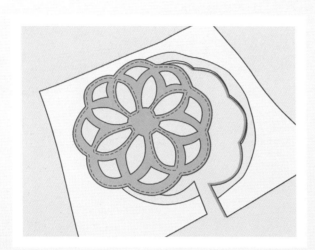

fig. A

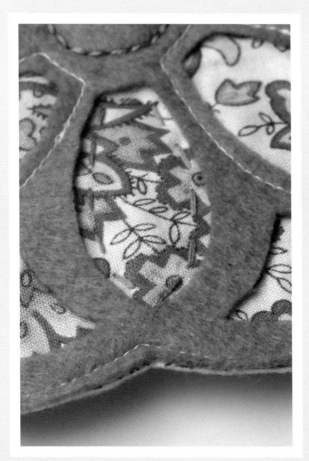

fig. B

6 Cut through the fabric and bottom felt layer following the outside edge of the top felt layer **(fig. A)**.

TIP
While you're cutting away the excess fabric and bottom felt layer, turn the scissors to a 45° angle so the bottom layers are cut slightly smaller than the top felt layer.

finishing

7 Using a coordinating floss and an embroidery needle, stitch a running stitch around the inside edge of the four petals you didn't stitch around in step 5.

8 Trace a bobbin in the center of the doily with a fabric marker. Using the same floss, backstitch around the circle **(fig. B)**.

variation!

Use your favorite crochet doily pattern as inspiration and make your own template.

25

baby BOOTIES

A small amount of felt is all you
need to cover up small feet.

designed by: *cynthia shaffer*

from your stash

2 pieces of felt, each 9 x 12 inches
(22.9 x 30.5 cm)

Piece of fabric, 9 x 9 inches
(22.9 x 22.9 cm)

gather

Basic felt sewing kit (page 7)

Template (page 117)

Matching or coordinating thread

Embroidery floss

Bobbin or other small circular
object, to trace

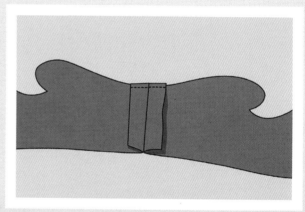

fig. A

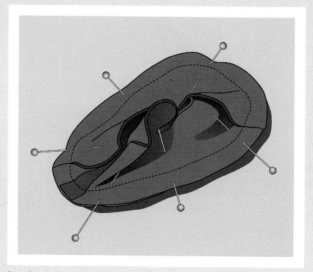

fig. B

fig. C

fig. D

make

❶ Trace the templates from page 117 onto the felt, and cut out two soles and two pairs of the upper shoe shapes.

❷ Transfer all template markings to the felt (needle-felted circles, eyelet placement, center front, and center back on all pattern pieces).

the left bootie

❸ Needle felt small circles wherever marked.

❹ Stitch the center back seam with a ⅜-inch (9.5 mm) seam allowance. Open the seam and stitch the seam allowance open close to the top cut edge **(fig. A)**.

❺ Pin the upper shoe parts together—overlapping the matching center front notch—and stitch in place.

❻ Pin a sole to the upper shoe, matching the center front and center back notches. Stitch together with a ⅜-inch (9.5 mm) seam allowance **(fig. B)**. Trim the seam to ⅛ inch (3 mm).

❼ Using white perle cotton, hand stitch around the needle-felted circles and the perimeter of the shoe, close to the edge. Add French knots to the center of the needle felted circles **(fig. C)**.

❽ Set two eyelets as desired and thread one piece of ribbon through the eyelets **(fig. D)**.

the right bootie

❾ Using the remaining felt pieces, follow steps 3 to 8 of the left bootie instructions to make the right bootie.

owly LUNCH BAG

With a reinforced bottom for added strength, this design is a sturdier version of a paper lunch sack.

designed by: *amanda carestio*

from your stash

1 yard (.9 m) of felt (main color), about 36 x 36 inches (91.4 x 91.4 cm)

Piece of brown felt, 9 x 12 inches (22.9 x 30.5 cm)

Small scrap of yellow felt

1 fat quarter of yellow fabric, about 18 x 22 inches (45.7 x 55.9 cm)

Piece of beige fabric (for owl body), 4 x 4 inches (10.2 x 10.2 cm)

gather

Basic felt sewing kit (page 7)

Templates (page 123)

Pinking shears

Matching thread

Piece of paper-backed fusible web, at least 4 x 4 inches (10.2 x 10.2 cm)

Brown thread

Brown embroidery floss

Button, 1 inch (2.5 cm) in diameter

make

the bag base

❶ Use the bag base diagram from page 123 to cut the main felt. Use pinking shears for the unmarked edges and sewing scissors on the indicated edge.

❷ From the remaining main felt, cut one 5½ x 8-inch (14 x 20.3 cm) piece and one 7 x 8-inch (17.8 x 20.3 cm) piece. Use pinking shears to trim the two short sides and one long side of the 7 x 8-inch (17.8 x 20.3 cm) piece.

❸ Pin the 5½ x 8-inch (14 x 20.3 cm) piece you just cut to the bottom center of the bag base and stitch it in place; this piece adds extra durability to the bottom of the lunch bag.

TIP
To reinforce the bag further, line the entire bag with your feature fabric or another fabric.

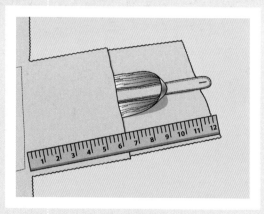

fig. A

fig. B

fig. C

the handle

❹ From the yellow fabric, cut a 3 x 9-inch (7.6 x 22.9 cm) strip. From the main felt, cut a 1½ x 9-inch (3.8 x 22.9 cm) strip.

❺ Fold under the long edges of the fabric strip. Center the felt strip on the wrong side of the fabric strip. Fold the fabric over the felt and stitch down. Stitch along the length of the strip two more times.

the strap

❻ Cut a 3 x 8-inch (7.6 x 20.3 cm) strip of fabric. Fold it in half with right sides together. Stitch along one long edge and one short edge, curving the short edge. Turn the strap inside out.

❼ Iron the strap and topstitch around the inside edge. Create a buttonhole in the curved end of the strap.

the back panel

❽ Pin the handle ends, with the strap between them, to the edge of the 7 x 8-inch (17.8 x 20.3 cm) piece you cut in step 2, aligning the raw edges with the straight cut edge of the rectangle.

❾ Lay the bag base down right side up and place the rectangle under the straight cut edge of the short panel. Overlap the edges so the combined length of the panel measures 12 inches (30.5 cm) **(fig. A)**. Pin and stitch in place, catching (and stitching a few extra times) over the raw edges of the handle and the straps.

❿ In each of the thinner sides of the bag base, stitch an upside-down Y shape to imitate a paper bag **(fig. B)**.

the front panel

⓫ Cut a 2 x 8-inch (5.1 x 20.3 cm) strip from the yellow fabric. Fold under and iron all the edges, and pin the strip in place on the right side of the Front Panel, about 1½ inches (3.8 cm) from the bottom edge of the panel. Stitch around the edge of the fabric panel.

⓬ Iron the fusible web to the back of the beige fabric. Trace the owl body template from page 123 onto the fusible-web-backed fabric square and cut out the shape. Trace the templates for the ears, wings, and feet onto the brown felt and cut out the shapes.

⓭ Fuse the owl body in place on top of the fabric strip using a pressing cloth. (You may want to test first to avoid melting your felt.) Stitch around the shape as close to the edge as possible.

⓮ Spray baste the back of the ears, wings, and feet shapes and place them on top of the body shape, using the photo as a guide. Hand stitch the shapes in place with brown thread. Using brown embroidery floss, backstitch V shapes to create eyes and stitch once over the nose to define the beak **(fig. C)**.

assembly

⓯ With wrong sides together, pin and stitch together the four sides of the bag at the edges.

⓰ Cut a circle of felt that is slightly larger than your button. Position the felt circle and the button in the center of the bag above the owl and stitch in place **(fig. D)**.

variation!

Use a different animal appliqué. Or make the bag a bit bigger and add two straps to create a mini backpack.

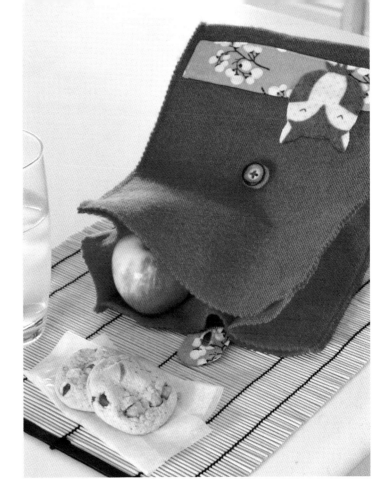

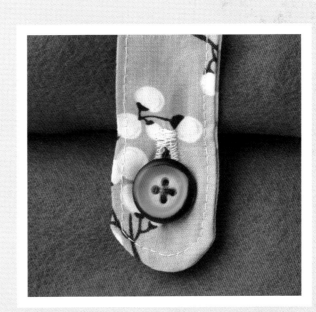

fig. D

felt blooms WREATH

Yarn and felt work together to make
this charming wall hanging.

designed by: *jennifer fitzsimmons*

from your stash

4 pieces of felt in assorted
colors, each 9 x 12 inches
(22.9 x 30.5 cm)

1 skein of yarn

gather

Basic felt sewing kit (page 7)

Straw wreath, 8 inches
(20.3 cm) in diameter

Hot glue gun

make

the yarn wreath

1 Wrap the wreath with yarn all the way around.

2 When you reach the point where you started, overlap the yarn, cut off the
extra yarn leaving a 2-inch (5.1 cm) yarn tail, and tuck in the tail to hide it.

the large flowers (make 4)

3 Cut four different colors of felt into sixteen circles, four per color, in the
following sizes: ¾ inch (1.9 cm) in diameter, 1½ inches (3.8 cm) in diameter,
2 inches (5.1 cm) in diameter, and 2½ inches (6.4 cm) in diameter.

4 Roll a ¾-inch (1.9-cm) circle into a tube and glue the shape in place. This
will create the inside of the flower.

5 Glue one of the ¾-inch (1.9-cm) circles around the middle piece **(fig. A)**.

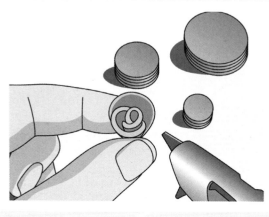

fig. A

fig. B

fig. C

fig. D

6 Cut off the remaining felt on the bottom of the flower to flatten the back **(fig. B)**.

7 Repeat step 5 two more times with ¾-inch (1.9-cm) circles. Continue adding layers, switching to the larger circles of felt as needed to get the desired flower structure. Make sure to cut off the excess circle material from the bottom as you go **(fig. C)**.

8 When you have reached the largest circle size for your flower, attach the petals in the same fashion, keeping in mind that this is the outside layer and the edges will be visible. Watch your placement.

the remaining flowers

9 Cut out more felt pieces as you did in step 3. However, for smaller size flowers you will need fewer 2-inch (5.1 cm) and 1½-inch (3.8 cm) diameter circles and can omit 2½-inch (6.4 cm) circles entirely.

10 Repeat steps 4 to 8 as for the large flowers to make as many smaller flowers as you like.

finishing

11 When you have made about eight to twelve flowers in several sizes, position them on the wreath to figure out how you would like them to be placed and to figure out how many more flowers, if any, you need to complete your arrangement **(fig. D)**.

12 Make additional flowers as needed. Once you are happy with the placement and your design looks balanced, use the hot glue gun to secure the flowers to the wreath.

variation!

Planning out your color scheme is key. Make a wreath to match the color of your door or to coordinate with other furnishings. Add some stripes by using variegated yarn or multiple colors.

carnation DECORATIONS

Make a few of these in a variety of colors and take them out whenever you have a party!

designed by: *catarina filipe*

from your stash

½ yard (0.5 m) of cream or white felt (small)

½ yard (0.5 m) of turquoise felt (medium)

¾ yard (75 cm) of lime green felt (large)

gather

Basic felt sewing kit (page 7)

Templates (page 120)

3¾ yards (3.4 m) of twine

Matching thread

make

one carnation

1 Trace the carnation template from page 120 onto the felt ten times. Use cream felt for the small carnation, turquoise felt for the medium carnation, and lime green felt for the large carnation. Cut out the shapes.

2 Cut the twine into a length appropriate for your chosen size: use 1 yard (.9 m) for the small, 1¼ yards (1.1 m) for the medium, and 1½ yards (1.4 m) for the large. Make a loop on one end of the twine and a simple knot on the other.

3 Sew the knot of the twine in the center of one circle. This will be the center piece of your carnation.

4 With another circle of felt, start making the "petals." Fold this circle in half and then in half again, so it is a quarter of a circle.

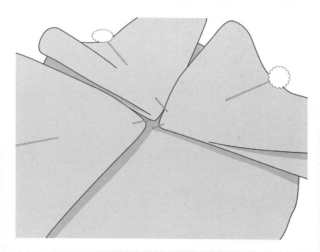

fig. A

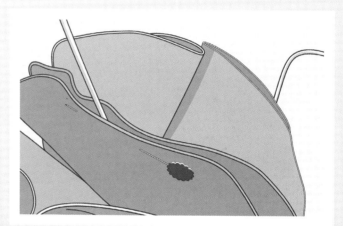

fig. B

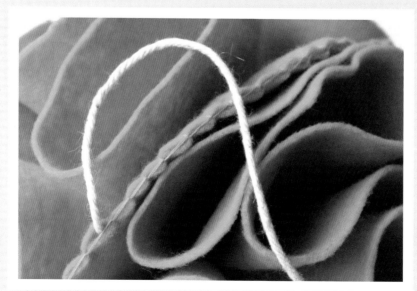

fig. C

⑤ Center the piece from step 4 on the center piece of your carnation. Make sure it is in the back of the knot of twine you sewed in place. Pin, then sew just the corner of it to the center piece **(fig. A)**.

⑥ Repeat steps 4 and 5 with another circle. This time when you attach it, match the open folds of the new quarter to the open folds on the quarter you just sewed.

⑦ Repeat steps 4 and 5 with another circle, matching the closed fold of this quarter circle to a closed fold of the petals already in place.

⑧ Repeat steps 4 and 5 again for the last petal on this half of the carnation. This time, attach the new quarter so that the opened and closed folds match.

⑨ Once you have the petals sewn in place, open them with your fingers and attach them to one another by sewing diagonally, about ½ inch (1.3 cm) above the center. This will keep the petals together and give the carnation its round shape.

⑩ Repeat steps 4 to 9 for the other half of the carnation (this side needs no twine).

⑪ Pin the finished carnation halves together on the top of the center circles. Pull the twine out at the top of the carnation **(fig. B)**.

⑫ To make sure your carnation keeps its shape, sew both pieces together in the center with two or three stitches. The sewing should not be visible or destroy the round effect of the petals.

⑬ Starting 1 inch (2.5 cm) away from the twine, blanket stitch around the edge of the center pieces **(fig. C)**.

variation!

Try using a longer piece of twine and make one single mobile with the three carnation sizes.

scrap COASTERS

These coasters will soak up your scraps, leftover batting, and extra lengths of embroidery floss.

designed by: *cathy ziegele*

from your stash

4 pieces of felt in assorted colors, each at least 4 x 4 inches (10.2 x 10.2 cm)

4 pieces of fabric in assorted colors, each at least 4 x 4 inches (10.2 x 10.2 cm)

8 pieces of cotton batting, each at least 4 x 4 inches (10.2 x 10.2 cm)

gather

Basic felt sewing kit (page 7)

Card stock

Matching thread

Circle template, assorted sizes

Embroidery floss

make

❶ Trace a circle template onto card stock and cut out the shape. Save the circle as well as the card stock with the circle missing. You will use this last piece as a window to see where to best cut your circle from the fabric **(fig. A)**.

TIP
You can make any size coaster you like, just use the same size template for all of your layers.

❷ Using a fabric marker and the inside edge of the card stock window, mark where you want to cut a circle

on your fabric, then cut out the shape. When you cut, stay to the outside of the line to make up the difference between the window and the actual circle template. The fabric you choose will be the anchor for all the colors you use for the rest of the project. Cut four of these circles for a set, or as many as you like.

❸ Using the card stock circle template, cut four coordinating circles from assorted colors of felt.

❹ Using the card stock circle template, cut eight circles of batting, two for each coaster (one for the front and one for the back).

❺ Assemble your coasters, with the batting in the middle of the fabric and felt layers, and baste them together.

fig. A

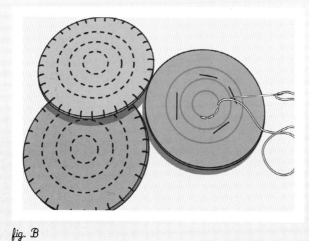

fig. B

fig. C

the embellishments

❻ Using the assorted circle template, draw three concentric circles on the felt side of each coaster (they will be easier to see on the solid color felt). My circles measured 2¼ inches (5.7 cm), 1⅝ inches (4.1 cm), and ¾ inch (1.9 cm) in diameter so they would be the same distance apart.

❼ Starting at the smallest circle, sew a running stitch in a contrasting color of embroidery floss following the lines you made in step 6 **(fig. B)**. Change the color of the floss with each circle using colors found in the fabric **(fig. C)**.

❽ To finish the coasters, sew a blanket stitch around the outer edge of each.

fox
BROOCHES

These furry felted friends
are perfect for your hats,
beanies, or scarves.

designed by: *karen de nardi*

from your stash

Felt scraps in orange

Felt scraps in contrasting color
(for ribbon or bow tie)

White adhesive felt

Black adhesive felt

gather

Basic felt sewing kit (page 7)

Templates (page 114)

¼-inch (6 mm) hole punch

1 yard of 6 strand embroidery
floss

Small handful of polyester
fiberfill for stuffing

Metal brooch pin

fig. A

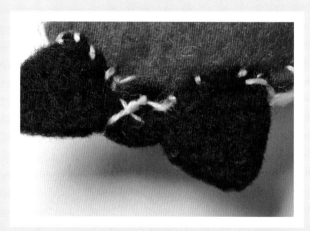

fig. B

make

1 Trace the head template from page 114 onto your chosen color of felt twice and cut out the shapes.

2 Trace the cheek template from page 114 onto the white adhesive felt twice and cut out the shapes.

3 Using the black adhesive felt, cut out a rectangle for the nose and two circles for the eyes.

TIP
To get an even shape for each eye, just use a hole punch.

4 Adhere the two cheek pieces, the eyes, and the nose in position on the front head piece. If you don't have adhesive felt you can use glue with your felt.

5 Using three strands of embroidery floss, make a French knot in the center of each eye to secure, without cutting your thread. Then push the thread through to the left edge of both head pieces, wrong sides together, and blanket stitch clockwise around the head to join the two pieces. Stop when you reach the nose.

6 Stuff your brooch as firmly as desired before completing the edge stitching. Push the remaining thread through to the back and stitch on the metal brooch pin **(fig. A)**.

7 Using the remaining strand of embroidery thread, complete your brooch by attaching the optional bow or bow tie **(fig. B)**.

variation!

If you want to make a wolf instead of a fox, cut two ear pieces in step 3 and adhere them in step 4. Oh, and don't forget to use gray felt instead of orange!

woven e~reader CASE

A simple weaving technique is used here—try the same idea for other electronics!

designed by: *ellen luckett baker*

from your stash

Piece of gray 2 mm felt, approximately 8½ x 11 inches (21.6 x 27.9 cm)

Piece of white 2 mm felt, approximately 8½ x 3 inches (21.6 x 7.6)

gather

Basic felt sewing kit (page 7)

Diagrams (page 115)

Matching thread

note:

The instructions that follow are for an e-reader that is approximately 4¾ x 7½ inches (12 x 19 cm). To adjust the felt cutting dimensions to fit your e-reader, measure your e-reader and add 1 inch (2.5 cm) vertically and 1½ inches (3.8 cm) horizontally. The seam allowance for this project is ⅛ inch (3 mm).

make

❶ Cut the white felt into three 1 x 8½-inch (2.5 x 21.6 cm) strips.

❷ Place the gray felt on the cutting mat and mark the lines on the back of the felt as shown on the cutting diagram (page 115).

❸ Using a rotary cutter, carefully cut slits along the marked lines. Flip the felt over so that the slits are still on the right side of the felt, but now on the front.

❹ With a 1-inch (2.5 cm) strip, weave over and under, through the slits. With the next strip, weave the opposite way. Then finish with the last strip, weaving over and under as you did with the first one. Pin in place at the edges if needed **(fig. A)**.

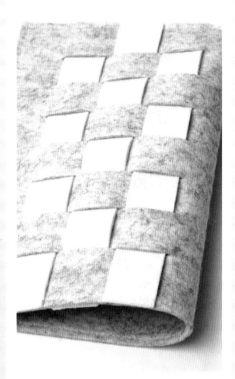

fig. A

fig. B

❺ Starting from the top left corner of the gray felt, sew a line across the top, ⅛ inch (3 mm) from the edge, to secure the top strips. You will start at the left corner so that the stitching will go all the way across the top of what will become the opening of the case **(fig. B)**.

❻ Fold the piece in half at its width, with the woven strips on the front of the felt piece. Pin in place if needed, and sew the piece together along the side and bottom, ⅛ inch (3 mm) from the edge using the assembly diagram (page 115) as a guide.

variation!

To make this project no-sew, just substitute glue for the stitches.

wine
TOTE

This sturdy bag
lets your wine or
champagne travel
first class.

designed by: *thom o'hearn*

from your stash

4 pieces of felt, each
12¾ x 6½ inches (32.4 x 16.5 cm)

4 pieces of felt, each
4 x 7 inches (10.2 x 17.8 cm)

2 pieces of fabric, each
12¾ x 6½ inches (32.4 x 16.5 cm)

2 pieces of fabric, each
4 x 7 inches (10.2 x 17.8 cm)

Scraps of felt or fabric

gather

Basic felt sewing kit (page 7)

Templates (page 114)

Embroidery floss

make

❶ Enlarge and trace the tote and handle templates from page 114 onto the felt pieces and cut out the shapes four times (you will have a double layer of felt pieces for each).

❷ Using the tote and handle templates, cut two tote pieces and two handle pieces from the fabric.

❸ Sew together two pieces of felt and one piece of fabric for each side of the tote and each of the two handles. A sewing machine is recommended for the strength of the stitches, but you can sew by hand **(fig. A)**.

fig. A

fig. B

④ If you would like to add a design with fabric or scrap felt, use embroidery floss to sew scraps onto the front or back tote body pieces **(fig. B)**.

⑤ Place one of the two tote handle pieces about ½ inch (1.3 cm) over the top of one of the two tote body pieces. Sew the pieces together.

⑥ Repeat step 5 with the remaining tote handle and tote body piece.

⑦ With right sides of the tote together, sew the bottom, left, and right sides up through where the handles attach. You may stop about ½ inch (1.3 cm) from the top so that the bag will open wider if needed.

variation!

This project can be even scrappier if you want. You can use different colors of felt for the body and the handles, or you can combine felt scraps to make the 12¾ x 6½-inch (32.4 x 16.5 cm) pieces of felt for the outside of the tote (like the Owl Plush Toy, page 56)!

whale
PINCUSHION

He'll be quite content to hold your pins and needles—just no harpoons, please!

designed by: *cathy gaubert*

from your stash

Piece of aqua felt (upper body and fins), 8 x 12 inches (20.3 x 30.5 cm)

Piece of white felt (underbelly), 7 x 7 inches (17.8 x 17.8 cm)

Piece of red felt (heart and fish), 4 x 4 inches (10.2 x 10.2 cm)

Piece of blue felt (waterspouts), 4 x 4 inches (10.2 x 10.2 cm)

gather

Basic felt sewing kit (page 7)

Templates (page 124)

6 flat head quilter's pins

Embroidery floss in black and red

Sewing thread in aqua and red

Wool or polyester stuffing

make

the whale

1 Trace the fin (twice), gusset, and side template from page 125 onto the aqua felt. Then trace the reverse of the side template. Make sure to mark the letters with a disappearing ink fabric marker on the gusset and sides: On the side piece, mark point B at the nose and point A at the tail end, and on the reversed side piece, mark point D at the nose and point C at the tail end. Cut out the shapes.

2 Match points A on the side and gusset. Stitch with an ⅛-inch (3 mm) seam allowance from A to B. You can snip off the excess at the front end once you have sewn both sides to the gusset.

3 Match points C on the reverse side and the gusset, and stitch from C to D. Trim the excess straight across.

4 Referring to the template for placement, stitch the eyes with four strands of black floss. With two strands of black floss, stitch the lashes **(fig. A)**.

5 Trace the underside template from page 125 onto the white felt and cut out the shape, making a slit that measures approximately 2½ inches (6.4 cm) (this is where you will insert the stuffing later). Transfer markings for the fins, where the gusset should match up, and mark point E.

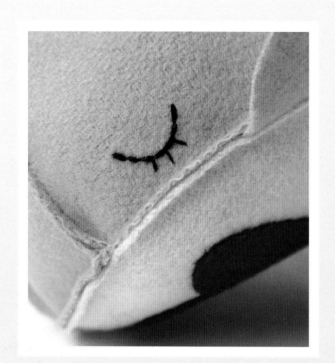

fig. A

fig. B

fig. C

fig. D

the pins

⑩ Using craft scissors, carefully snip off the three sides of the flat head quilter's pins, leaving a little bit of the plastic surrounding the top of the pin.

⑪ Trace the waterspout templates from page 124 onto the blue felt and cut out the three waterspouts. Sandwich one pin between a spout and the remaining blue felt. Carefully stitch together the spout and felt close to the edge of the spout shape, enclosing the pinhead. Trim the felt along the edges of the spout **(fig. C)**.

⑫ Repeat step 11 to make the remaining two spouts.

⑬ Trace the fish templates from page 124 onto the red felt two times and cut out three of the six traced pieces. Embroider an eye on each piece, making sure to create matching sets. Assemble the three matching fish pins together. Trim the felt along the edges of the fish **(fig. D)**.

⑭ Poke the pins into the whale, and you've got yourself a handy pincushion. Or you can keep the pins out and have a cute new softie for the kiddos.

⑥ Tack the fins into place on the underbelly with a few basting stitches, leaving long tails so that the stitches can be pulled out later.

⑦ Matching points E on the gusset and underbelly, carefully stitch from point E around one side of the tail, the body, and then the other side of the tail, ending where you began.

⑧ Stuff firmly with wool or polyester stuffing. Close the opening with a few stitches.

⑨ Trace the heart templates from page 124 onto the red felt and cut out the shape. Place the heart on the belly, covering up the now-closed opening. Using two strands of red embroidery floss, attach the heart to the belly **(fig. B)**.

owl PLUSH TOY

Who doesn't love a new
felt-feathered friend?

designed by: *aimee ray*

from your stash

Felt scraps in assorted colors

gather

Basic felt sewing kit (page 7)

Templates (page 116)

Embroidery floss

Pinking shears

Buttons, colored fabric, or other embellishments

White chalk

Polyester stuffing

make

❶ Trace the template of your choice (small or large) from page 116 onto paper and cut it out. Don't worry about being too precise: A wonky shape gives these owls more character.

❷ Assemble your scraps. This is a little like putting together a puzzle. You can cut them down to the shape you need if necessary. Roughly organize them into a shape big enough to cover your template, plus about ½ inch (1.3 cm) around all edges. Repeat for the reverse side **(fig. A)**.

❸ Start stitching your pieces together. Pick up a scrap and the one next to it, overlap them ¼ to ½ inch (6 mm to 1.3 cm), and sew them together using embroidery floss and a whipstitch (the overlap is important since it will keep your stuffing from leaking out) **(fig. B)**.

TIP
Don't worry about making it too neat! The charm of scrappy stuffed toys is that they're totally unique.

fig. A

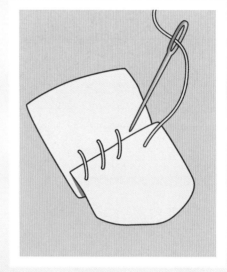

fig. B

fig. C

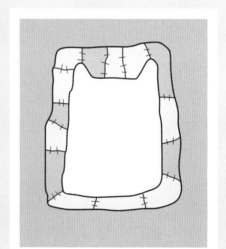

fig. D

❹ Stitch another scrap to the last one, using the same technique as step 3. Keep stitching until all scraps are sewn together securely.

the embellishments

❺ When you've got two pieces of patchwork felt big enough to cover your template, determine which piece to use as the front. Add the face or other decorations to this piece.

❻ For the eyes, cut two circles out of fabric with pinking shears, sew a button in the middle of each, and stitch them to the front panel **(fig. C).**

❼ For the nose, cut a small triangle from felt and hand stitch it in place between the eyes.

assembly

❽ Pin the front and back pieces together, right sides facing, and trace the template onto the felt with white chalk **(fig. D)**. Sew around the edges following this outline, leaving the bottom open.

❾ Cut off the excess seam allowance. Turn the owl right side out, stuff, and sew up the opening.

mushroom
TERRARIUM

Felted wool sweater scraps turn into
a needle-felted nature scene.

designed by: *lisa jordan*

from your stash

Scraps of thick felted white
wool sweater

Scraps of lightweight white
felt, as from a blazer or pair
of pants

Wool roving in white, brown,
dark brown, moss green,
and gray

Wool yarn (optional)

gather

Basic felt sewing kit (page 7)

Felting needles in sizes 38
and 40

Felting foam

Glass apothecary jar, jelly jar,
or candle jar

make

the mushrooms

❶ Form stems for your mushrooms
by wrapping strips of the felted
sweater with white roving and
needle felting using a size 38 needle.
Continue to add layers of roving until
you have the desired shape and the
stem is firm enough to support the
weight of its cap. Be sure to make the
stem long enough to be seated down
into the base of the scene by about
½ inch (1.3 cm).

❷ Cut a doughnut-shaped piece
of the felted sweater, making the
center hole just large enough for
the mushroom stem to fit through.
This will become the base for your
mushroom gills.

❸ Cut several strips of the
lightweight felt into pieces about
½ x 1 inch (1.3 x 2.5 cm). These will
become the gills for your mushroom.

❹ Place the doughnut shape on
the felting foam. Using a size 40
needle, carefully needle down the
middle of one of the white strips
until it begins to felt to the base.
The edges of the strip will begin to
naturally fold upward as the center
becomes securely felted. Once the
piece is secure, repeat the process
with another strip directly across
from the first. Continue to fill in the
entire base with gill strips **(figs. A,
B, & C)**.

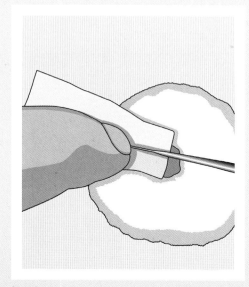

fig. A

fig. B

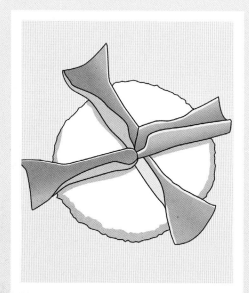

fig. C

fig. D

fig. E

fig. F

5 Trim the gills to sit flush with the outside diameter of the gill base and to be of a uniform height **(fig. D)**.

6 Insert the mushroom stem through the hole in the gill base and needle it to secure it to the base **(fig. E)**.

7 Cut a circle of felted sweater slightly smaller than the gill base. Wrap the piece in brown roving, place it on the felting foam, and needle it until the roving has covered the piece entirely. This is the beginning of your mushroom cap. Place this piece on the gill base and carefully needle it in place, taking care not to push the needle all the way through to the gills. Once the piece is tacked in place, wrap brown roving around the edge of the cap, and needle it into place to cover the exposed gill edges. Continue to needle the brown roving around the edge and over the top of the cap until you've achieved the desired size and shape **(fig. F)**.

8 Repeat steps 1 to 7 to create a second mushroom. If desired, form the second mushroom smaller and without the gills.

the scene

9 Cut out two circles from the felted sweater, using the glass jar as a template. One circle should be the same size as the bottom of your jar, and one should be slightly smaller. (If you're not using a jar, cut the pieces to the size and shape you would like for a base.)

10 Stack the two base pieces, wrap them in dark brown roving, place them on the felting foam, and needle them together until the piece is uniformly covered. This will create the dirt in your scene and the base for your mushrooms. Check to be sure the base fits firmly into your jar. If it doesn't, you can needle the base into shape or add more roving until it fits. If desired, needle gray roving into pebble shapes and attach them to the bottom of the base.

11 Wrap moss green roving around the outside of the base and needle it into place, leaving the top of the base uncovered.

12 Designate the spots where your mushrooms will be planted and cut small, shallow holes in the top of the base to accommodate them. Needle the mushroom stems into the holes. Continue wrapping and needle felting moss green wool around the base and mushroom stems until the base is covered and the mushroom stems are secure.

13 Add details to your piece by using scrap pieces of felted wool and wool yarn. Wrap gray roving around small pieces of felted sweater and needle it to form stones. Cut thin pieces of roving into leaf shapes. A small scrap of wool yarn can be needled to the leaf to act as a stem. Needle these details directly to the base. Small scraps of wool can also be needled beneath the moss layer to add height and interest **(fig. G)**.

14 Place your completed scene into the jar, pressing firmly into place.

fig. G

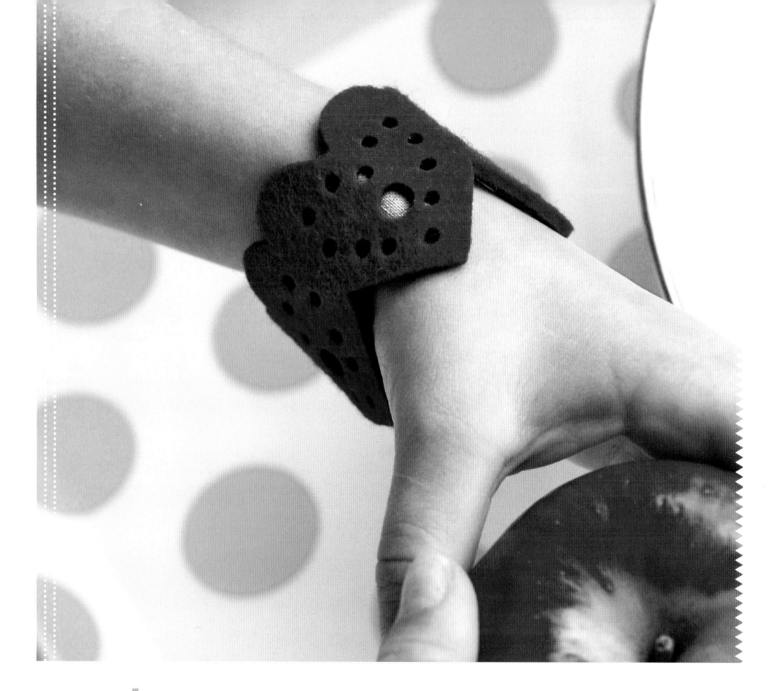

heart BRACELET

With just a scrap of red felt and some fabric,
this charming accessory is a snap to make!

designed by: *ellen luckett baker*

from your stash

Piece of 2 mm felt, 2 x 6 inches
(5.1 x 15.2 cm)

Piece of backing fabric, 2 x 6 inches
(5.1 x 15.2 cm)

gather

Basic felt sewing kit (page 7)

Templates (page 121)

⅛ inch (3 mm) mini hole punch

¼ inch (6 mm) hole punch
(standard size)

2 to 4 inches (5.1 to 10.2 cm) of elastic

Matching thread

make

① Trace the bracelet template you wish to use from page 121 onto the felt and fabric and cut out the shapes. When cutting the felt, it's helpful to pin the template paper directly onto the felt and use a pair of small, sharp scissors.

② With the template still pinned to your felt, punch the holes as indicated. First make the smaller holes, then punch the larger holes in the center of the design **(fig. A)**.

③ Place small dots of fabric glue along the edges of the backing fabric and adhere it to the back of the felt. Allow the glue to dry for at least an hour before starting the next step.

④ Measure the elastic and adjust it so that the bracelet will fit the wrist (it should slip on and off easily). Cut the elastic accordingly and sew it to the back of the bracelet at both ends, using a straight stitch **(fig. B)**.

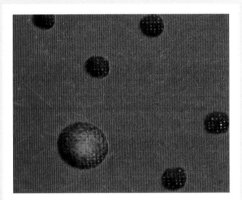

fig. A

fig. B

variation!

Add embellishments like embroidery or beading or cut intricate designs into the felt with a craft knife.

really raccoon
T-SHIRT

Only three scraps of felt
can transform this shirt
for your little critter.

designed by: *mary rasch*

from your stash

Black machine-washable felt,
5 x 12 inches (12.7 x 30.5 cm)

2 pieces of tan machine-washable felt, 7 x 10 inches
(17.8 x 25.4 cm) and about
6 x 6 inches (15.2 x 15.2 cm)

gather

Basic felt sewing kit (page 7)

Templates (page 119)

White T-shirt

Iron and ironing board

Light brown embroidery floss

make

1 Prepare the T-shirt by machine washing and drying it to avoid further shrinking after your project is complete. Iron out any wrinkles.

2 Trace the templates from page 119 onto the black (piece B) and tan felt (pieces A, C, & D), and cut out the shapes.

3 Apply glue to the wrong side of the tan oval tummy piece (piece A). Center this piece on the front of the shirt and set it in place. Starting at the center of the oval, press firmly and continue outward. Allow the glue to fully dry before continuing.

4 Apply glue to the wrong side of the black tail piece (piece B). Center this piece on the back of the shirt horizontally with the bottom edges aligned and set in place. Starting at the center of the tail, press firmly and continue outward.

5 Apply glue to the wrong sides of the tan tail stripes (pieces C and D). Place these pieces on the black tail piece using the photos as a guide and press firmly. Allow the glue to fully dry before continuing.

6 Finish by topstitching with the brown embroidery floss around the inside of the tummy, tail, and tail stripes **(figs. A & B)**.

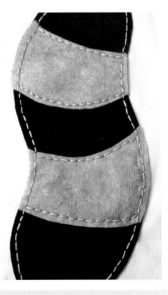

fig. A

fig. B

retro CLUTCH

Just a little bit of felt
makes for a whole lot
of style.

designed by: *amanda carestio*

from your stash

Two pieces of sturdy felt, each
9 x 12 inches (22.9 x 30.5 cm)

¼ yard (.23 m) of fabric

Sheet of coordinating felt, 9 x 12
inches (22.9 x 30.5 cm)

gather

Basic felt sewing kit (page 7)

Template (page 114)

Matching thread

Store-bought purse clasp

Vintage button

make

❶ From the sturdy felt, cut one
piece 4½ x 9 inches (11.4 x 22.9 cm)
and one piece 9 x 9 inches (22.9 x
22.9 cm).

❷ From the fabric, cut one piece
5½ x 9 inches (14 x 22.9 cm) and one
piece 9 x 9 inches (22.9 x 22.9 cm).

the front panel

❸ Spray baste together the smaller
sections of felt and fabric with wrong
sides facing, leaving the extra inch
(2.5 cm) of fabric at the top edge.

❹ Cut two 4½ x ½-inch
(11.4 x 1.3 cm) strips from the
coordinating felt. Spray baste,
position, and stitch them to the felt
side of the front panel.

❺ Trace the clasp template from
page 114 onto the coordinating
felt twice. Cut one shape to the full
length and one to the line indicated
on the template. Put the shorter
piece aside for now. Spray baste and
position the full-length piece in the
center of the panel and stitch in place
(fig. A).

❻ Fold the extra fabric over the edge
twice (catching the raw edges of the
strips and clasp template piece), pin,
and stitch in place.

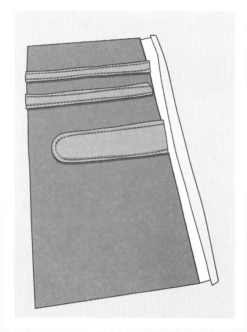

fig. A

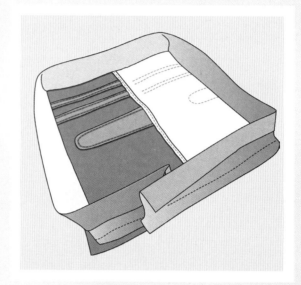

fig. B

fig. C

the back panel

 Spray baste together the larger sections of felt and fabric with the wrong sides facing and the edges aligned.

⑧ Cut two 9 x ½-inch (22.9 x 1.3 cm) strips from the coordinating felt. Spray baste and position them on the felt side of the back panel so that they line up with the strips on the front panel when the clutch is folded. Stitch the strips in place.

⑨ Spray baste and position the shorter purse clasp template piece from step 5 at the center top edge of the back panel, making sure it lines up with the piece on the front panel when the clutch is folded. Stitch the clasp template piece in place.

assembly

⑩ Line up the bottom raw edges of the front and back panels with wrong sides facing. Stitch the pieces together along the left, bottom, and right edges.

⑪ Cut or piece together 2½ inch-wide (6.4 cm) strips of fabric for binding. You'll need about 45 inches (114 cm) total. Iron under each long edge of the binding ¼ inch (6 mm), and then iron the binding in half lengthwise.

⑫ Working from the front of the clutch, stitch the binding to the raw edge with right sides together **(fig. B)**. Fold the binding over, and stitch it to the back of the clutch **(fig. C)**.

TIP
If you have enough coordinating felt, you can use it as binding instead of using the fabric.

⑬ Attach the purse clasp to the center of the front panel **(fig. D)** and to the center or the back panel where they should meet.

⑭ Fold the clutch over and attach the button at the top center.

variation!

Personalize your clutch with felt hexagons (like in the Hexy Stocking on page 19), felt zigzag strips, cut felt initials, or a cute appliqué shape (like the owl in the Owly Lunch Bag on page 28).

fig. D

cutie CROWN

Make your felt into an accessory
fit for a queen!

designed by: cynthia shaffer

from your stash

¼ yard (.23 m) off-white felt

¼ yard (.23 m) light blue felt

Scraps of purple felt

gather

Basic felt sewing kit (page 7)

Template (page 114)

Matching thread

Gesso

Paint brush

Page from an old book

Pencil

Fine tip white paint marker

White embroidery floss

16 white buttons

80 inches (203 cm) of off-white ribbon, ½ inch (1.3 cm) wide

make

1 Trace the crown template from page 114 onto the off-white felt and cut out the shape.

2 Using the felt crown piece as a template, cut out a crown piece from the light blue felt, adding ¼ inch (6 mm) around the perimeter for a border.

3 Stitch around the perimeter of the two crown pieces to secure the layers together.

the embellishments

4 Paint gesso on the book page and set it aside to dry.

5 Using a pencil, trace the circle template from page 114 onto the gessoed book page five times and cut out the shapes, leaving the pencil marks showing if you'd like. Add small dots around the circles with a white paint marker.

6 Place the circles on the crown. Stitch them in place, and stitch around the outer edges of the circles (fig. A).

7 Trace the flower template from page 114 onto the light blue felt four times and cut out the shapes. Cut four small circles from the purple felt.

8 Using embroidery floss, stitch the center of the felt flowers in place with three French knots (fig. B).

9 Stitch the buttons in place as desired (fig. C).

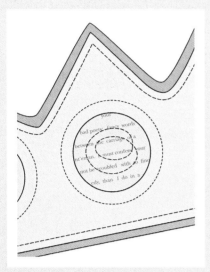

fig. A

fig. B

fig. C

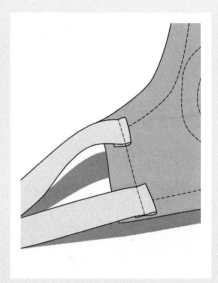

fig. D

the ties

⑩ Cut four 20-inch (50.8 cm) lengths of off-white ribbon.

⑪ Fold the ends of the ribbon under ½ inch (1.3 cm), pin to the back opening of the crown, and stitch in place **(fig. D)**.

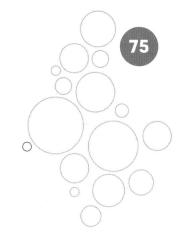
circles
SCARF

Warmer than
a necklace but
smaller than the
average scarf.

designed by: *cynthia shaffer*

from your stash

1 felted wool sweater
(Instructions for Machine
Felting Your Sweater,
page 10)

Off-white felt scrap

gather

Basic felt sewing kit
(page 7)

Templates (page 117)

Matching thread

make

❶ Trace the circle template from page 117 onto the felted sweater thirty times
and cut out the shapes.

❷ Overlap two circles by 1 inch (2.5 cm) and stitch them together in a serpentine
pattern **(fig. A)** (also see the stitch pattern on page 117).

❸ Repeat step 2 until all but four circles are attached.

❹ Overlap two of the remaining circles and stitch them together. Working on
one end of the scarf, stitch the attached circles onto the third circle from the end.
Repeat with the remaining two circles at the other end of the scarf.

fig. A

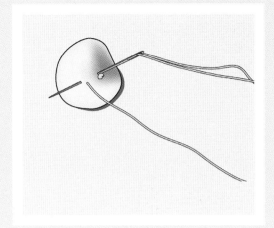

fig. B

fig. C

the flowers

5 Trace the flower template from page 117 onto the felted sweater twice and cut out the shapes.

6 Using a hand sewing needle, stitch a running stitch along the curved edges of each flower.

7 Pull the stitches to gather the edges, roll each flower into itself, and sew back and forth through the base to secure.

8 Cut two small circles, each about the size of a quarter, from off-white felt.

9 Pinch each circle in the middle and stitch the pinched felt to itself to secure the shapes. **(fig. B)**.

10 Stitch a pinched circle to the center of each felt flower **(fig. C)**.

11 Tack a flower to each end of the scarf where you attached the extra circles (see step 4).

woolen tree TRIO

What a sweet, green family
of felt and wool trees!

designed by: *lindy cline*

from your stash

Felt scraps in grays and greens
Green wool roving
Green wool yarn

gather

Basic felt sewing kit (page 7)
Template (page 120)
3 foam cones (various sizes)
Felting needle
Pinking shears

make

the small tree

1 Glue the bottom of the smallest cone to a piece of gray felt. Once the glue is dry, trim closely around the cone with scissors. This will finish the bottom of your tree **(fig. A)**.

2 Pull off a small strip of wool roving. Hold the wool against the cone. Starting at the bottom of the cone, use the felting needle to poke the wool into the cone. Make sure to stick the needle through the wool until you enter the foam.

3 Continue to poke the wool in a concentrated area until the wool attaches to the cone. Move around the bottom of the cone, pulling off more pieces of roving as necessary. Continue to attach the wool to the cone, moving around the cone up to the tip. If you find any bald spots, pull off a small amount of roving and attach it.

fig. A

fig. B

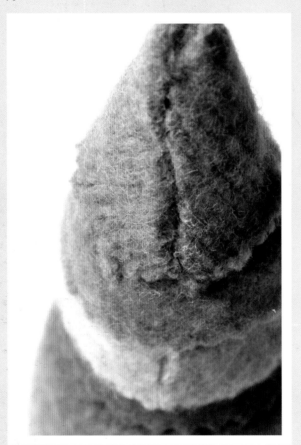

fig. C

fig. D

the medium tree

1. Glue the bottom of the medium-size cone to a piece of gray felt. Once the glue is dry, trim closely around the cone with scissors. This will finish the bottom of your tree **(fig. A)**.

2. Cut strips of felt in various colors about 1 x 8 inches (2.5 x 20.3 cm). The size of the strips doesn't need to be exact. Cut one side of the strip using pinking shears to create a zigzag pattern.

3. Spread glue around the bottom inch (2.5 cm) of the cone. With the zigzag edge towards the bottom, press one of the strips around the cone, gluing it in place. Trim the piece of felt so the two ends meet. You may want to use straight pins to hold the ends in place until the glue dries **(fig. B)**.

4. Glue the next strip with about ¼ inch (6 mm) overlapping the first strip, again with the zigzag edge pointed down. This will leave about ¾ inch (1.9 cm) of the first strip still showing.

5. Continue to glue overlapping strips until you reach the top of the cone.

6. Trace the template from page 120 onto a piece of felt and cut out the shape for the top of the tree. Trim the curved edge with pinking shears. Glue the shape around the tree top and trim off any excess **(fig. C)**.

the large tree

1. Glue the bottom of the largest cone to a piece of gray felt. Once the glue is dry, trim closely around the cone with scissors. This will finish the bottom of your tree **(fig. A)**.

2. Run a bead of glue from the bottom of the cone straight to the tip.

3. Leaving about a 1-inch (2.5 cm) tail, start from the initial glue spot and wrap the yarn around the cone. Keep wrapping the yarn as close to the last wrap as possible, covering all of the foam. Every time another wrap is made, the bead of glue will help keep it in place. You will find the yarn naturally wants to stick to the foam material.

4. Continue wrapping the yarn around the cone until you reach the top. Secure the top with another bead of glue. When the glue is dry, trim the yarn **(fig. D)**.

5. Use a bead of glue to finish the bottom tail. When it is dry, trim the yarn.

felt-framed PORTRAITS

These imaginative scenes can brighten up your wall or your desk.

designed by: *cathy gaubert*

from your stash

Pieces of wool felt in gray, light pink, dark pink, aqua, auburn, peach, and white, 5 x 7 inches (12.7 x 17.8 cm) or smaller

Piece of toile fabric, 5 x 7 inches (12.7 x 17.8 cm)

gather

Basic felt sewing kit (page 7)

Templates (page 122)

Piece of paper-backed fusible web

Embroidery floss in orange, black, pink, cream, blue, and lime green

make

the girl

❶ Trace the appropriate templates from page 122 onto the paper side of the fusible web and cut out the shapes, leaving approximately a border of about ¼ inch (6 mm) around each.

❷ Following the manufacturer's directions, iron each template piece onto appropriately colored felt. Set aside.

❸ Iron a piece of fusible web onto the back side of the toile fabric.

❹ Cut out a 5 x 7 inch (12.7 x 17.8 cm) piece of felt. Remove the paper backing from the toile fabric and iron the toile onto this piece of felt.

❺ Remove the paper backing from the felt frame piece and iron it onto the toile fabric. Do not trim the toile and felt backing.

❻ Gather all of the pieces for the girl. Remove the paper backing from all of the pieces, and assemble the girl on the toile in this order: legs, dress, hand (slid a little bit under the sleeve), collar, face, hair, and bird.

TIP
Fussy cut the piece of toile you'd like to feature in your background.

fig. A

❼ Carefully iron all pieces and let cool.

❽ Using two strands of the appropriate embroidery floss (for the eyes, however, use only one), create the hair in orange; the eyes, lashes, and stockings in black; the dress and lips in pink; the collar in cream; the bird in blue; and the bird's beak in orange using the following stitches: running stitch, backstitch, satin stitch, French knots. For the stocking legs, simply stitch across the stocking to hold the leg in place, beginning under the dress and ending at the ankle. Use satin stitch to make the shoes and the bird's beak **(figs. A & B)**.

❾ Using a running stitch, secure the inner edge of the frame to the toile and felt backing.

fig. B

the embellishments

⑩ Freehand cut four hearts, four medium circles, four large circles, and four simple leaf shapes to decorate the frame.

⑪ To make the two flowers on the frame, snip two of the large circles along the edge to create the petals. Square off two of the medium circles for the center of the flowers. Assemble the flowers with three French knots through the centers of the flowers. Attach the hearts to the frame with three French knots. Attach the finished flowers to the frame with a single cross stitch, and the leaves with a single long stitch.

⑫ Trim the toile and felt backing to match the frame's edge.

fig. C

the bird

⑬ Follow steps 1 to 4 of the girl instructions.

⑭ Remove the paper backing from the felt frame piece. Create the cut-outs in the frame by folding each scallop in half and making a V-shaped cut (two quick snips). Do not trim the toile and backing.

⑮ Gather all of the pieces for the bird. Remove the paper backing from all of the pieces, and assemble the bird onto the toile. Iron and let cool.

⑯ Using two strands of the appropriate embroidery floss, hand stitch the following elements as follows: the bird in blue; the eyes and lashes in black; the legs and beak in orange; the stem and hill in lime green **(fig. C)**; and the flowers in yellow and pink.

⑰ Follow steps 9 to 12 of the girl instructions to finish the frame.

scrap story
BOOKMARK

These make a great gift
for the wee bookworm
in your life.

designed by: *aimee ray*

from your stash

Long, thin felt and fabric scraps in assorted colors

gather

Basic felt sewing kit (page 7)

Embroidery patterns (page 116)

Embroidery floss

Pinking shears (optional)

Ribbon, ¼ to ½ inch (6 mm to 1.3 cm) wide

make

❶ Cut a strip of felt and a strip of fabric to the size you want for the large, back piece of the bookmark. You can cut these strips in varying sizes and shapes and even use pinking shears if you'd like. To make a bookmark as shown, cut each back piece to measure 1½ x 8 inches (3.8 x 20.3 cm).

❷ Cut another piece of felt or fabric slightly smaller, about ½ inch (1.3 cm) thinner and ½ inch shorter (1.3 cm) than the back pieces.

❸ Embellish the top layer using the embroidery pattern from page 116 and floss. Just measure the size of pattern that you need, and then draw or transfer the embroidery pattern to the top fabric piece **(fig. A)**.

❹ Place the embellished piece on top of the back pieces and pin them together.

❺ Cut a piece of ribbon to the desired length and place it between the layers at one end **(fig. B)**.

❻ Stitch the pieces together with embroidery floss. Start the knot between the layers to hide it and make sure to stitch the ribbon in place securely.

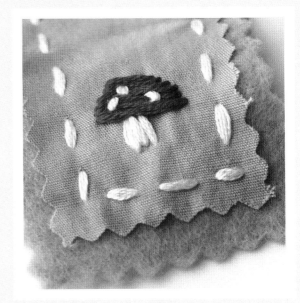

fig. A

fig. B

beary baby
HAT

The ears on this hat make it an adorable accessory for your little one.

designed by: *mary rasch*

from your stash

1 felted wool sweater
(Instructions for Machine Felting
Your Sweater, page 10)

gather

Basic felt sewing kit (page 7)

Templates (page 118)

Matching thread

Embroidery floss in
complementary color

make

❶ Trace the hat template from page 118 onto the felted sweater, lining up the template with the finished edge at the bottom of the sweater **(fig. A)**. Pin the template to the sweater and cut out the shape twice. Trace, pin, and cut out two ear pieces using the ear template from page 118.

❷ On the two ear pieces, use a running stitch approximately ¼ inch (6 mm) from the edge to create an accent for the inner ear **(fig. B)**.

❸ Pin the two hat pieces together with right sides together. Sandwich the ears in place using the template as a guide. Make sure to have the ears on the inside, pointing down, so the bottom of the ears line up with the raw edges on the seam.

❹ Machine or hand stitch around the edge of the hat, using a ¼ inch (6 mm) seam allowance.

❺ Turn the hat right side out. If you didn't use a finished edge on the bottom of your hat (as mentioned in step 1), fold up the bottom edge to create a cuff and hand sew in place.

fig. A

TIP
If you would prefer, you can use any part of the sweater, just add an extra inch (2.5 cm) to the bottom of the template to allow for a finished edge **(fig. A)**.

fig. B

variation!

With a simple switch of the ear shape or placement, this hat can look more like a cat, bunny, or even a monkey. See the additional ear templates on page 118.

trees please
SEWING MACHINE COZY

Some simple appliqué trees make

this project a woodsy delight.

designed by: *amanda carestio*

from your stash

Piece of felt, 15 x 24 inches
(38.1 x 61 cm)

8 pieces of felt in 4 shades of
brown and green, each 3 x 3
inches to 4 x 4 inches (7.6 x 7.6
cm to 10.2 x 10.2 cm)

Piece of coordinating fabric,
17 x 26 inches (43.2 x 66 cm)

gather

Basic felt sewing kit (page 7)

Templates (page 119)

Pinking shears (optional)

Matching thread

4 grommets and grommet
setter

2 yards (1.8 m) of cording

make

❶ Spray baste the back of the large felt piece and center it on the back of the
fabric piece, with an extra inch (2.5 cm) of fabric along each edge.

❷ Working on the long edges, fold the extra fabric in half and then over the
edge of the felt. Pin and stitch in place.

❸ Working on the short edges, fold the extra fabric in half and then over the
edge of the felt. Fold the ends under (creating butted corners), pin, and stitch in
place **(fig. A)**.

fig. A

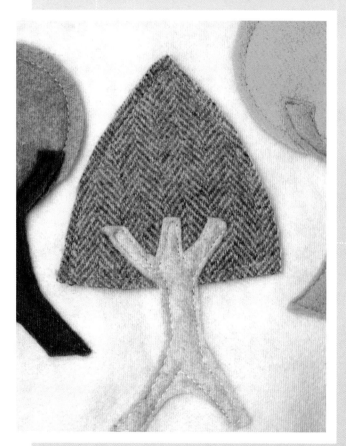

fig. B

fig. C

the appliqué

4 Trace the trunk template from page 119 onto each piece of brown felt and the tree templates onto each piece of green felt. Use sharp scissors or pinking shears to cut out the shapes, introducing variations as you cut.

5 Spray baste the backs of the tree shapes and position them above the short edge of your panel (this will become the front of the cozy). Machine stitch them in place.

TIP
To keep your felt shapes from moving as you stitch them in place, try using spray baste and pins. You can also lighten the pressure on your presser foot.

6 Spray baste the backs of the trunk shapes and position them on the panel, overlapping the tree shapes. Stitch them in place **(fig B)**.

finish

7 Set a grommet in each side edge of the panel, about 2 inches (5.1 cm) from the bottom and ½ inch (1.3 cm) from the edge.

8 Cut the cording in half. To create the tabs, cut four 2 x ½-inch (5.1 x 1.3 cm) rectangles from green felt. Fold and pin the rectangles over each raw end of the cording and stitch in place **(fig. C)**.

9 Feed the cording through the grommets and tie in a bow.

mismatched MITTENS

A mix of colors and repurposed felt make these mittens unique and unexpected.

designed by: *lindy cline*

from your stash

3 felted wool sweaters (Instructions for Machine Felting Your Sweater, page 10)

gather

Basic felt sewing kit (page 7)

Templates (page 126)

Thread

make

1 Cut apart the felted sweaters. You should cut the side and shoulder seams of the body, the seam of the sleeve, and the ribbing of the sleeve (cut about an inch above the edge of the ribbing). Save the ribbing pieces, you will need them.

2 Depending on how much the sweaters shrunk during felting, you should have four fairly good-sized pieces to work with. Your mittens won't use up all the material, so you'll have some more felt for your stash.

3 Trace the templates from page 126, pin them to the material, and cut out the shapes. The same pattern piece can be used for the right and left hands by simply turning it over to reverse. You will need to cut two backs, fingers, palms, and pieces of ribbing.

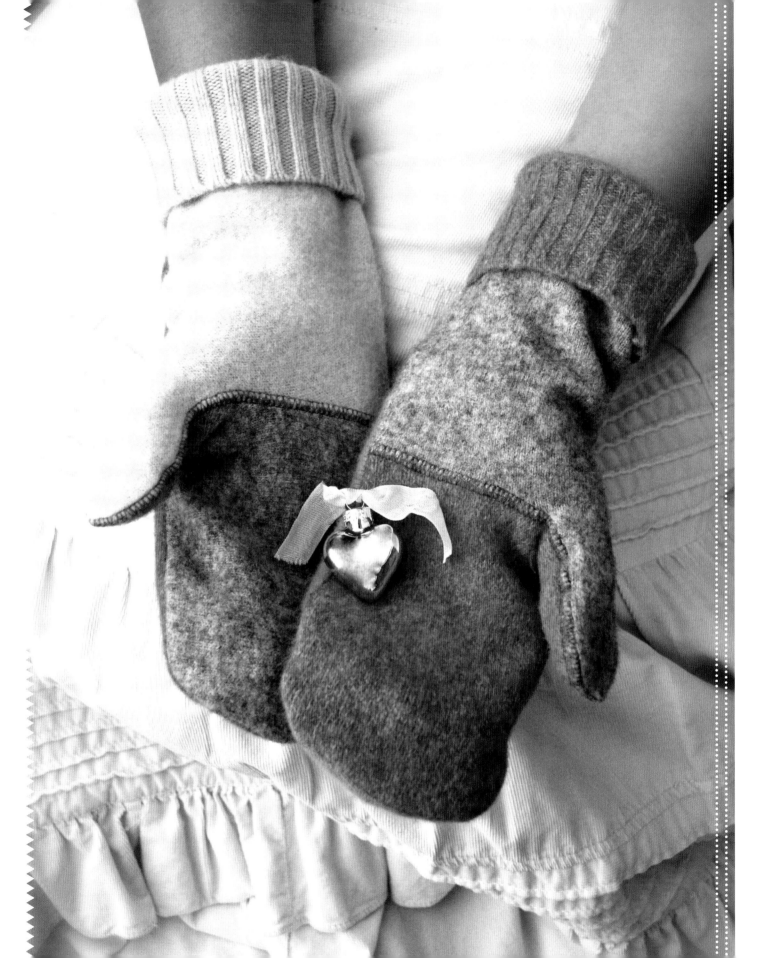

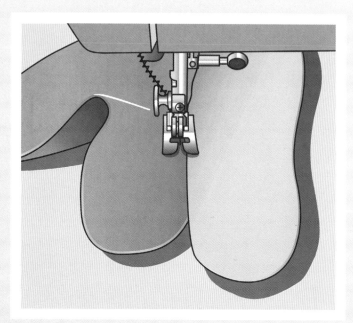

fig. A

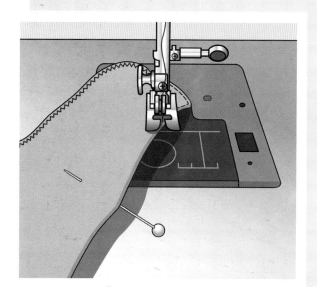

fig. B

fig. C

the hand

❹ Place the two left hand pieces against each other (non-thumb sides) and lay them in the sewing machine centered under the presser foot.

❺ Start sewing a zigzag seam through both pieces, slowing as you near the thumb.

❻ Reposition the felt so that the two sides of the thumb are next to each other. Continue the seam up the side of the thumb, pulling the fabric so the pieces are butted up to each other down the middle of the presser foot as you go **(fig. A)**. After you round the top of the thumb you will no longer be able to pull the fabric together—this is where your seam ends.

❼ Fold the fabric on the seam that you made in step 4, right sides together. Pin the two pieces with one pin that marks the bottom of the thumb.

❽ Use a straight stitch to sew the thumb down to the pin. Curve the seam toward the edge of the fabric and trim the threads **(fig. B)**.

❾ With the thumb inside out, pin the palm to the back piece, right sides together.

❿ Using a seam allowance of ¼ inch (6 mm), stitch a straight seam from the bottom, up and around the curve of the hand, and down the other side. When you near the thumb, flatten the thumb seam so the seam you are sewing can catch all of the thumb.

the cuff

⓫ Fold the ribbing in half and sew together, wrong sides facing.

⓬ Turn the mitten and ribbing right side out. Place the ribbing inside of the mitten (the right side of the ribbing will be against the wrong side of the mitten). Place the finished edge of the ribbing down so that the cut edge and the bottom of the mitten will be pinned together. Pin the ribbing in four places.

⓭ Using a seam allowance of ¼ inch (6 mm), sew around the cuff. Pull out the ribbing and press the seam open. Fold the cuff over **(fig. C)**.

⓮ Repeat steps 4 to 13 for the right mitten.

⓯ Trim the seams and press your new mittens with a warm iron.

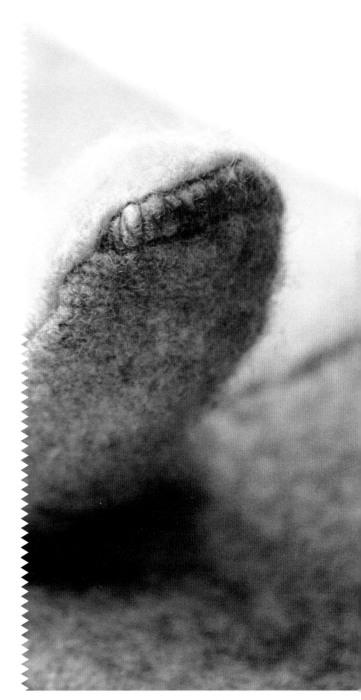

wallflower POCKET

This cute hanger uses felt as binding, making it strong enough for lots of mail, your keys, or whatever you need to keep handy!

designed by: *amanda carestio*

from your stash

Piece of cream felt, 20 x 20 inches (50.8 x 50.8 cm)

Three 20-inch (50.8 cm) strips of green felt (or enough to piece three strips together), 1 inch (2.5 cm) wide

Felt scraps in green, pink, yellow, and brown

Piece of fabric, 20 x 20 inches (50.8 x 50.8 cm)

gather

Basic felt sewing kit (page 7)

Templates (page 117)

Matching thread

Embroidery floss

2 grommets and grommet setter

make

the base

❶ Trace template A from page 117 onto the cream felt. Trace this template onto the fabric, adding an extra 1½ inches (3.8 cm) to the short center edge. Cut out the shapes.

❷ Trace template B from page 117 onto the cream felt twice, once as is and once in reverse. Trace this template onto the fabric twice, adding an extra 1½ inches (3.8 cm) along the top straight edge. Cut out the shapes.

❸ Spray baste the felt B pieces to the fabric B pieces, wrong sides together. Fold over the top edges of the fabric twice. Pin and stitch in place. Follow the same steps for the template A pieces, folding over the excess fabric on short center edge.

the front

❹ Trace the flower templates from page 117 onto the felt scraps as follows: one flower shape onto pink felt, one flower shape onto brown felt, two flower centers onto yellow felt, and four leaf shapes onto green felt. Cut out the shapes.

❺ Spray baste the backs of all the shapes and position them on template A, using the photo as a guide.

❻ Machine stitch the flowers and two of the leaves in place. Hand stitch the flower centers and the center of each leaf using a backstitch.

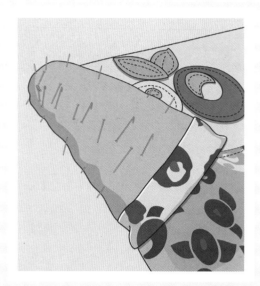

fig. A

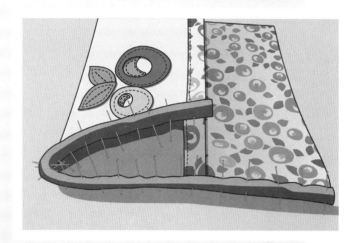

fig. B

fig. C

fig. D

assembly

7 Pin one side piece B to the base with the wrong sides together. Stitch the pieces together **(fig. A)**, working as close to the edge as possible. Repeat for the other side piece B.

8 Cut or piece together three 20 x 1-inch (50.8 x 2.5cm) strips of green felt to use as binding. Fold the binding in half.

9 Pin a binding strip in place over the raw edges where you attached the base and side pieces **(fig. B)**, and stitch it in place. Leave a little extra binding at the front end; hand stitch the binding to itself where it overlaps the edge of the base. Repeat for the other raw edge.

10 Using the technique in step 9, attach binding to the top edge of the pocket and finish the ends **(fig. C)**.

11 Position the two remaining leaf shapes on the top center of the pocket. Machine stitch around each shape and hand stitch through each center **(fig. D)**.

12 Set grommets in each corner.

variation!

Create your own appliqué shapes for the front of the pocket using your lining fabric as inspiration.

pretty pink GIFT TAG

Make a gift tag worth saving and reusing as a holiday ornament!

designed by: *cathy ziegele*

from your stash

Pieces of felt in rose and light pink, each 4 x 5 inches (10.2 x 12.7 cm)

Pieces of felt in light green and dark green, each 2 x 3 inches (5.1 x 7.6 cm)

gather

Basic felt sewing kit (page 7)

Templates (page 116)

Piece of card stock for each tag, 4 x 5 inches (10.2 x 12.7 cm)

¼-inch (6 mm) hole punch (optional)

Thread in white or a neutral color

Embroidery floss in light green, dark green, light pink, hot pink, and red

Computer and printer, or decorative paper crafting supplies (optional)

Double-sided tape

12 inches (30.5 cm) of ribbon, about ¼ inch (6 mm) wide

make

the pieces

❶ Trace the tag template from page 116 onto card stock and cut out the shape.

❷ Punch out the holes on the template, then trace the outline onto the rose felt. Using a fabric marker, make dots in the cut out circles for the flower placement guide **(fig. A)**.

❸ Enlarge and trace the petal template from page 116 onto the light pink felt eighteen times. Cut out the petals. **(fig. B)**

TIP
You can complete step 3 faster by cutting a few ¼ x 3 inch (6 mm x 7.6 cm) strips, then cutting them crosswise to make ¼ x ⅝ inch (1.6 cm) rectangles. Using craft scissors, round off the corners of the rectangles starting at the bottom and cutting upward.

fig. A

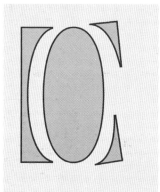

fig. B

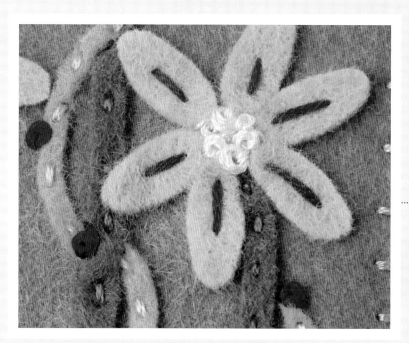

fig. C

4 To make flower stems, cut three strips of dark green felt no wider than a scant ¼ inch (6 mm) at the bottom and tapering to ⅛ inch (3 mm) at the top. To make vines, repeat using three strips of light green felt, but keep the light green felt strips closer to ⅛ inch (3 mm) throughout, with just a slight increase at the bottom.

5 Lay out your petals on the rose felt. Use the marks you made as the flower centers and leave that space open. Baste the petals with sewing thread.

6 Place the dark green stems on the rose felt, thin end at the petals, and loosely baste them. Trim off any excess stem.

7 Arrange the light green vines as shown, loosening the basting on the dark green stem to slip the vine underneath. Baste these as well and trim any excess felt.

8 Using only two strands of embroidery floss, stitch a running stitch to attach the stems with dark green floss and the vines with light green floss. Sew a single, but firm, stitch into each of the petals with two strands of hot pink floss.

9 Fill the center of your flower with five or six French knots using three strands of light pink floss. Using three strands of red floss, dot the vine with French knots as shown **(fig. C)**.

assembly
10 Personalize the card stock template for the back of the tag, if desired.

11 Cut down the card stock template you have been using by trimming ¾ inch (9.5 mm) off the sides and bottom, but leaving the rounded top alone.

12 Using double-sided tape, sandwich together the card stock back and felt top.

13 Using a blanket stitch, sew your tag together with three strands of light green floss.

14 Punch a hole at the top of your tag. Cut a 6-inch (15.2 cm) length of ribbon and thread it through the hole as a tie.

online!

Download instructions for a purple gift tag variation at www.larkcrafts.com/bonus.

nesting
BUCKETS

A favorite shape for quilters adds some
interest to these felt storage containers.

designed by: *amanda carestio*

from your stash

¼ yard (.23 m) of cream felt

3 strips of felt in coordinating
colors (or 3 strips of scrap-
pieced felt), each 8 x 20 inches
(20.3 x 50.8 cm)

¼ yard (.23 m) of total fabric

gather

Basic felt sewing kit
(page 7)

Templates (page 122)

Cream thread

Matching and coordinating
thread

Pinking shears (optional)

make

1 Cut the cream felt to create
7-inch-wide strips (17.8 cm) in 12-,
14-, and 16-inch (30.5, 35.6, 40.6 cm)
lengths. Cut fabric to match, and spray
baste the layers together with wrong
sides facing to create
three panels.

2 Working on your 12-inch (30.5
cm) panel from step 1, stitch vertical
lines (about 1½ inches [3.8 cm] apart)
through the layers with cream thread.
Stitch three or four horizontal lines
through the layers, alternating the
spacing. Then stitch a few lines of

vertical stitches through the center of
the piece using contrasting thread.

3 Use the template (page 122) and
pinking shears to cut a plus sign from
one of your coordinating felt strips.

4 Spray baste and stitch the plus sign
to the center of the panel **(fig. A)**.

5 Square up the edges of the felt and
the fabric by trimming off any excess.
With right sides facing, bring the two
short ends together. Pin and zigzag
stitch over the edge.

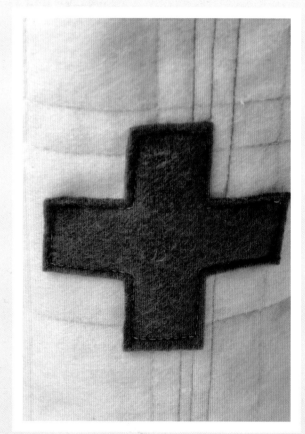

fig. A

fig. B

fig. C

the shaping and binding

6 Using felt to match your plus sign, cut a circle 4 inches (10.2 cm) in diameter. For the 14-inch (35.6 cm) panel, you'll need a circle 4¾ inches (12 cm) in diameter, and for the 16-inch (40.6 cm) panel, you'll need a circle 5¼ inches (13.3 cm) in diameter. While the cylinder is still inside out, pin the circle to the bottom edge. Stitch the cylinder to the circle, working as close to the edge as possible.

⑦ Turn the cylinder right side out. Cut a 1½ x 16-inch (3.8 x 40.6 cm) binding strip from a coordinating felt, using pinking shears on one edge. For the 14-inch (35.6 cm) panel, you'll need a binding strip 18 inches (45.7 cm) long, and for the 16-inch (40.6 cm) panel, you'll need a binding strip 20 inches (50.8 cm) long.

TIP
If your felt isn't long enough, simply piece scraps together using a zigzag stitch.

⑧ Pin the strip to the top edge of the cylinder with the sheared edge on the outside. Stitch around the edge to attach the binding strip **(fig. B)**.

⑨ Cut a 2½ x 5-inch (6.4 x 12.7 cm) tab from your coordinating felt. For the 14-inch (35.6 cm) panel, you'll need a tab 6 inches (15.2 cm) long, and for the 16-inch (40.6 cm) panel, you'll need a tab 7 inches (13.3 cm) long. Fold the tab in half and stitch the long edges together.

⑩ Fold the tab around to create a loop, and cut off the ends so the edge is straight **(fig. C)**. Stitch the tab to the back of the bucket with a zigzag stitch.

⑪ Repeat steps 2 to 10 using the other two panels and the appropriate measurements as indicated.

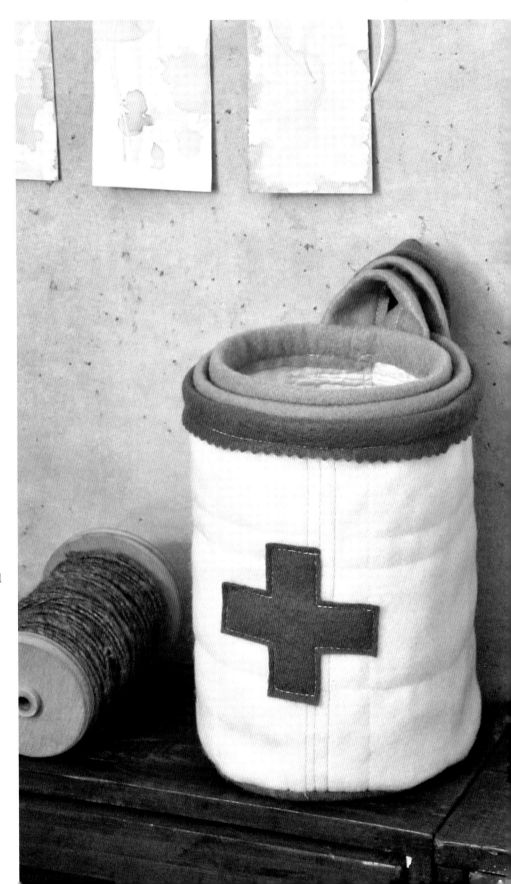

woodland
BEAR

Felt and fabric pieces too small to wear can turn into a bear!

designed by: *savannah carroll*

from your stash

2 pieces of felt (main color), each at least 6 x 12 inches (15.2 x 30.5 cm)

2 pieces of felt (coordinating color), each 6 x 6 inches (15.2 x 15.2 cm)

2 pieces of felt (second coordinating color), each 3 x 3 inches (7.6 x 7.6 cm)

gather

Basic felt sewing kit (page 7)

Templates (page 120)

Matching thread

Safety eyes and nose with washers

Embroidery floss

Polyester stuffing

make

① Trace the templates from page 120 onto the felt and cut them out. You can use whatever colors you like, but this design works best if you use three different colors for the body, belly/face, and eyes.

② Sew the face mask onto the front of the body first, then sew on the ears and eye patches.

③ Sew the belly onto the front of the body. It should overlap the felt between the legs slightly **(fig. A)**.

fig. A

fig. B

4 Cut small holes where the safety eyes will go. Flip the front of the body over and attach the safety eyes using a washer on the back.

5 Cut a small hole where the safety nose will go. Flip the front of the body over and attach the safety nose using a washer on the back.

6 Embroider the mouth, eyebrows, and freckles as shown **(fig. B)**.

assembly

7 With right sides together, pin the entire body. Sew, leaving a ¼ inch (6 mm) seam allowance. Leave a 2 to 3-inch (5.1 to 7.6 cm) opening between the ears for stuffing. Snip the seam allowance along the curvy edges.

8 Turn the bear right side out and stuff the entire body.

9 Stitch the opening closed.

templates

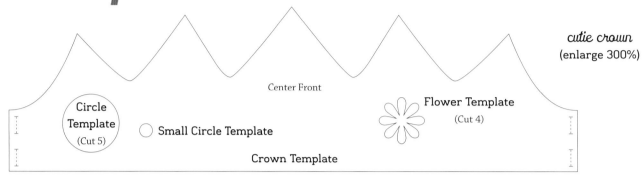

cutie crown
(enlarge 300%)

Center Front

Circle
Template
(Cut 5)

○ Small Circle Template

Flower Template
(Cut 4)

Crown Template

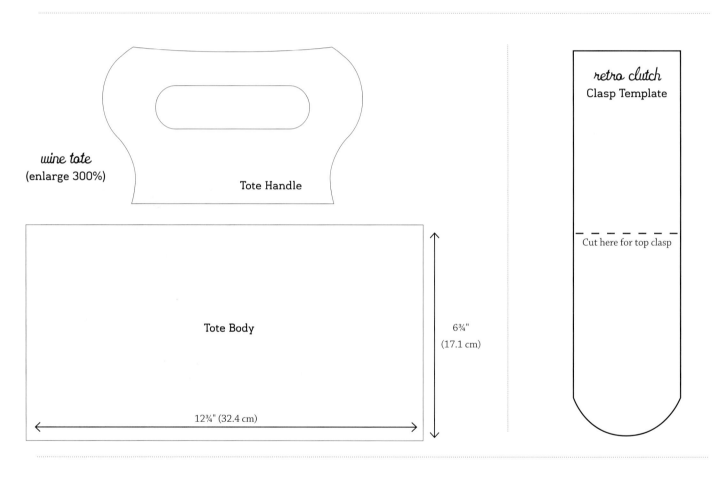

wine tote
(enlarge 300%)

Tote Handle

Tote Body

6¾"
(17.1 cm)

12¾" (32.4 cm)

retro clutch
Clasp Template

Cut here for top clasp

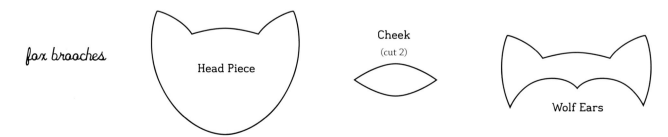

fox brooches

Head Piece

Cheek
(cut 2)

Wolf Ears

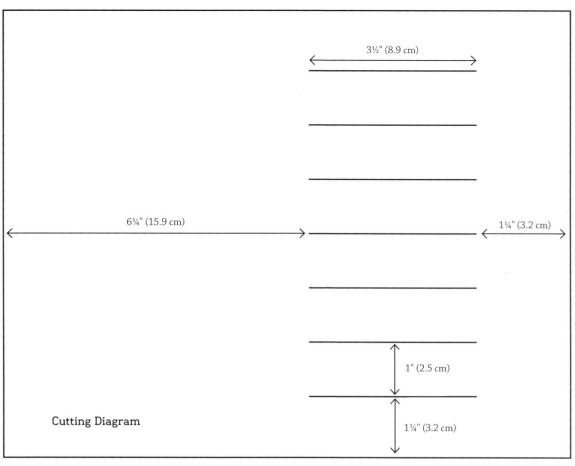

3½" (8.9 cm)

6¼" (15.9 cm)

1¼" (3.2 cm)

1" (2.5 cm)

1¼" (3.2 cm)

Cutting Diagram

woven e-reader case

Assembly Diagram

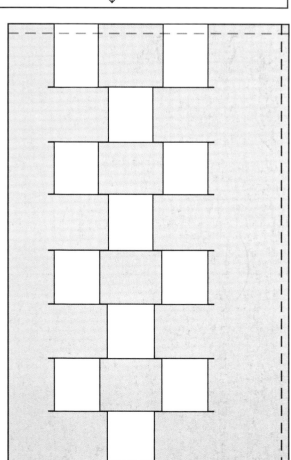

owl plush toy
(enlarge 300%)

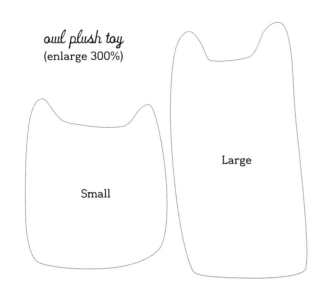

Small

Large

scrap story bookmark

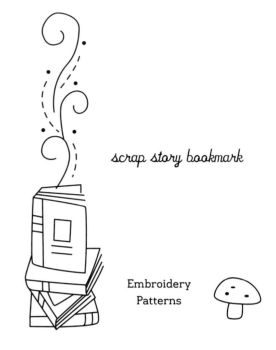

Embroidery
Patterns

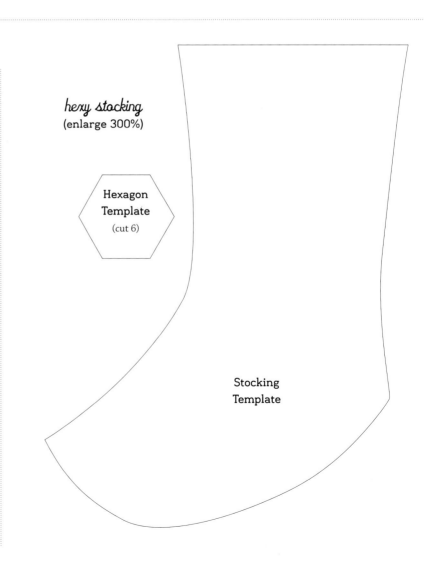

Template

hexy stocking
(enlarge 300%)

Hexagon
Template
(cut 6)

Stocking
Template

**pretty pink
gift tag**
(enlarge
200%)

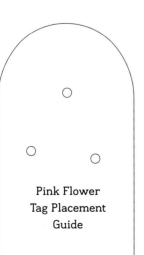

Pink Flower
Tag Placement
Guide

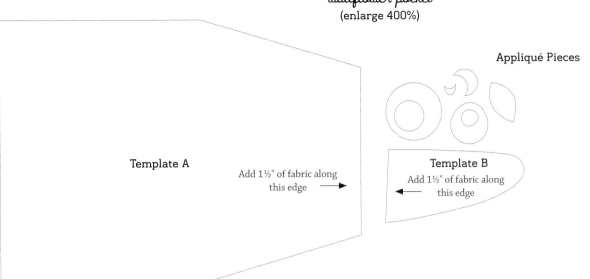

wallflower pocket
(enlarge 400%)

Appliqué Pieces

Template A

Add 1½" of fabric along
this edge →

Template B

Add 1½" of fabric along
this edge ←

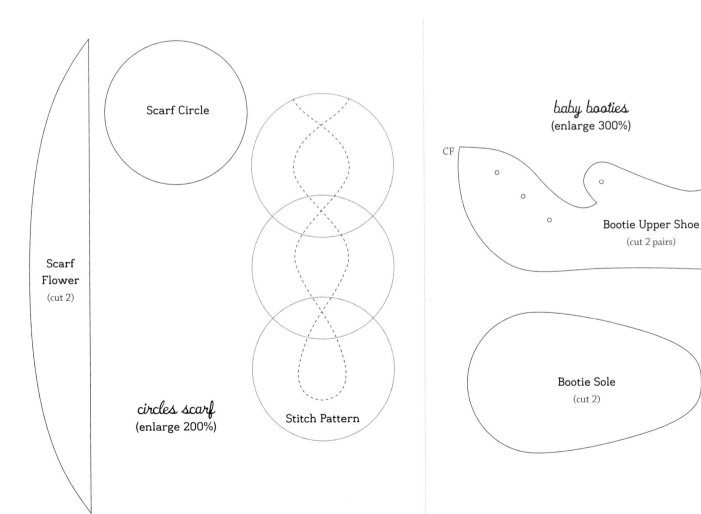

Scarf Circle

Scarf
Flower
(cut 2)

circles scarf
(enlarge 200%)

Stitch Pattern

baby booties
(enlarge 300%)

CF

Bootie Upper Shoe

(cut 2 pairs)

CB

Bootie Sole

(cut 2)

beary baby hat
(enlarge 300%)

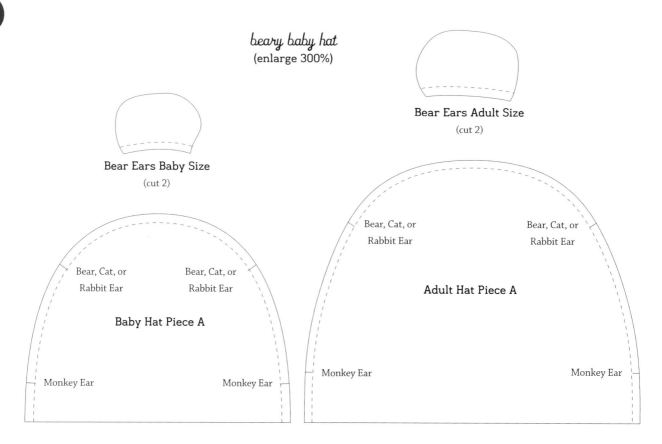

Bear Ears Baby Size
(cut 2)

Bear Ears Adult Size
(cut 2)

Bear, Cat, or
Rabbit Ear

Bear, Cat, or
Rabbit Ear

Baby Hat Piece A

Bear, Cat, or
Rabbit Ear

Bear, Cat, or
Rabbit Ear

Adult Hat Piece A

Monkey Ear

Monkey Ear

Monkey Ear

Monkey Ear

Variations
(enlarge 300%)

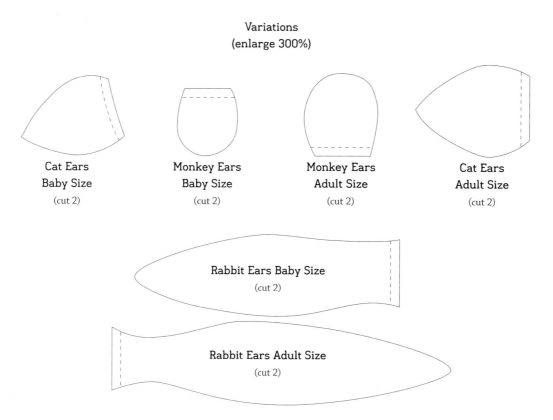

Cat Ears
Baby Size
(cut 2)

Monkey Ears
Baby Size
(cut 2)

Monkey Ears
Adult Size
(cut 2)

Cat Ears
Adult Size
(cut 2)

Rabbit Ears Baby Size
(cut 2)

Rabbit Ears Adult Size
(cut 2)

really raccoon t-shirt
(enlarge 200%)

Piece A
(cut 1)

vintage trivet
(enlarge 300%)

(cut 1)

Piece D
(cut 1)

Piece B
(cut 1)

Piece C
(cut 1)

trees please
sewing machine cozy
(enlarge 200%)

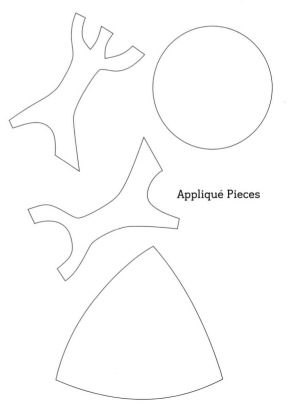

Appliqué Pieces

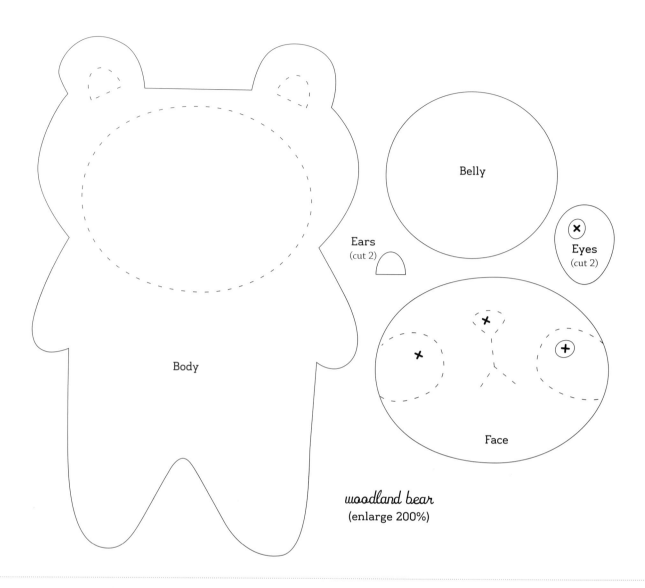

Belly

Ears
(cut 2)

Eyes
(cut 2)

Body

Face

woodland bear
(enlarge 200%)

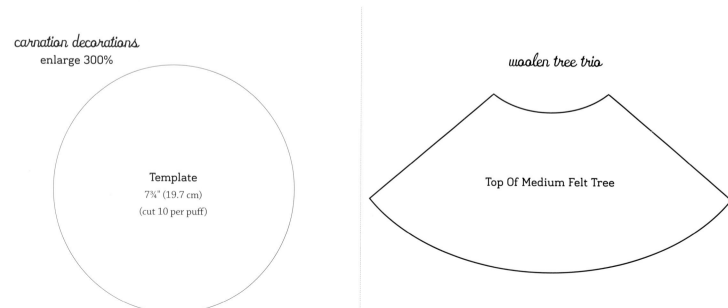

carnation decorations
enlarge 300%

Template
7¾" (19.7 cm)
(cut 10 per puff)

woolen tree trio

Top Of Medium Felt Tree

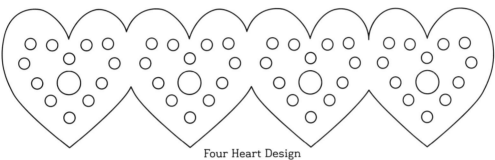

Four Heart Design

(cut 1 from fabric)

Four Heart Design

(cut 1 from felt)

Three Heart Design

(cut 1 from fabric)

Three Heart Design

(cut 1 from felt)

stash happy FELT

felt-framed portraits
Templates

nesting buckets

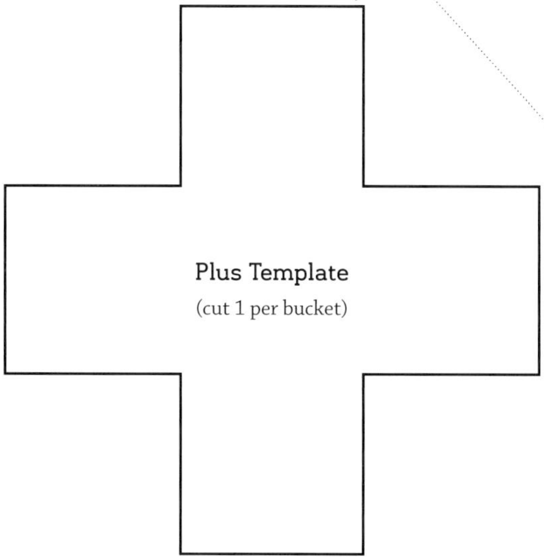

Plus Template
(cut 1 per bucket)

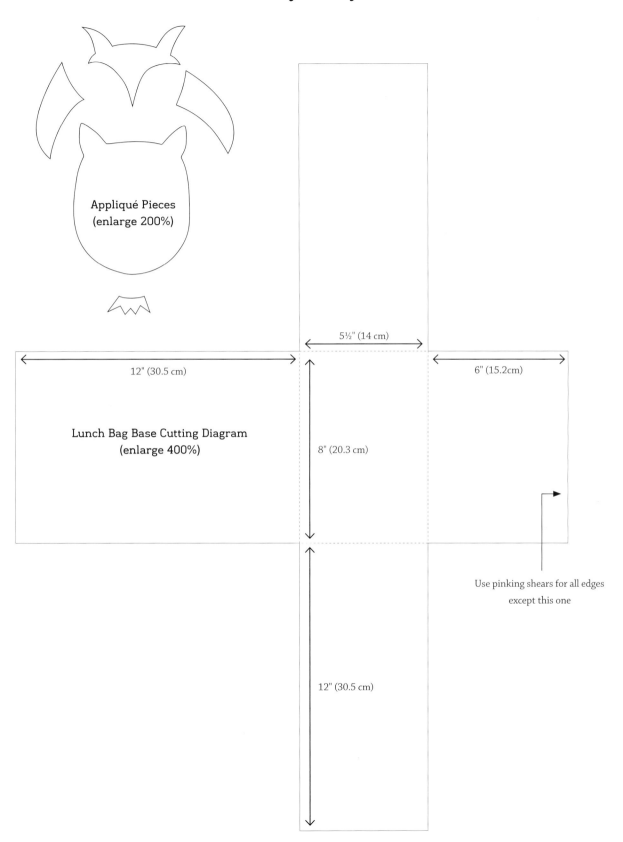

Appliqué Pieces
(enlarge 200%)

5½" (14 cm)

12" (30.5 cm)

6" (15.2cm)

Lunch Bag Base Cutting Diagram
(enlarge 400%)

8" (20.3 cm)

Use pinking shears for all edges
except this one

12" (30.5 cm)

whale pincushion

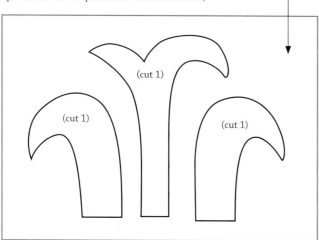

Waterspout Pin Toppers
(piece of felt to sew pieces onto and then cut out)

(cut 1)

(cut 1)

(cut 1)

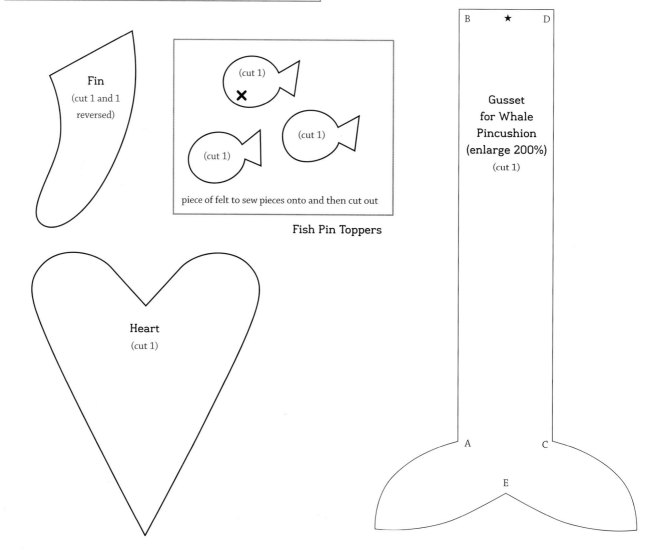

Fin
(cut 1 and 1 reversed)

(cut 1)

(cut 1)

(cut 1)

piece of felt to sew pieces onto and then cut out

Fish Pin Toppers

Heart
(cut 1)

B ★ D

Gusset for Whale Pincushion (enlarge 200%)
(cut 1)

A C

E

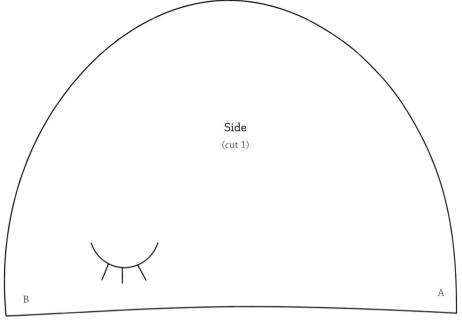

Side
(cut 1)

B

A

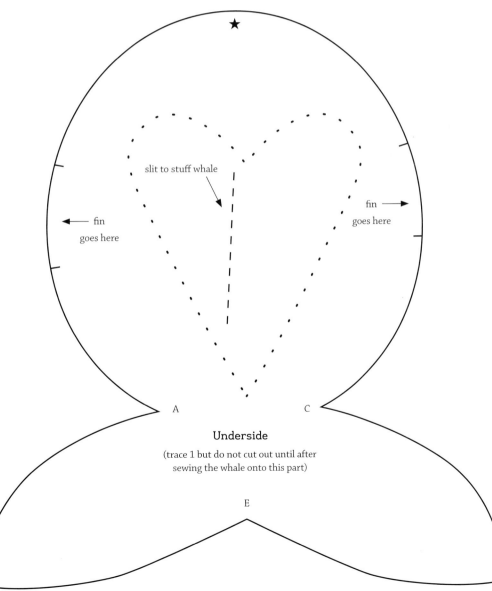

★

slit to stuff whale

fin
goes here

fin
goes here

A

C

Underside
(trace 1 but do not cut out until after
sewing the whale onto this part)

E

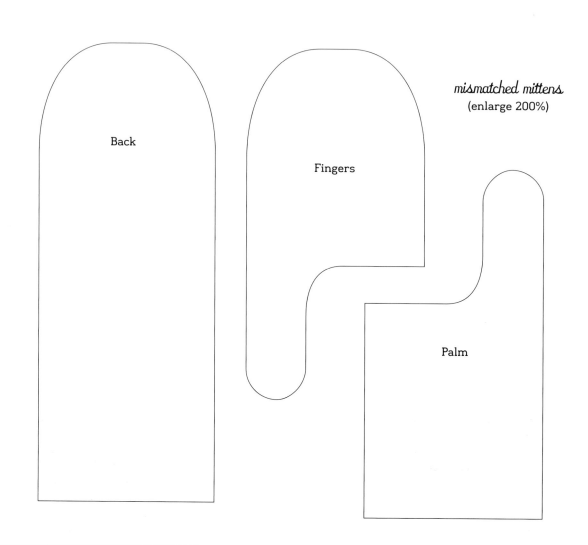

mismatched mittens
(enlarge 200%)

Back

Fingers

Palm

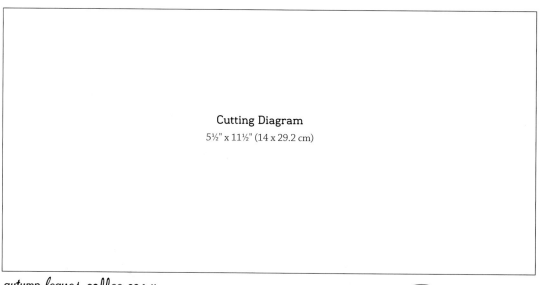

Cutting Diagram
5½" x 11½" (14 x 29.2 cm)

autumn leaves coffee cozy
(enlarge 200%)

Leaf Template
(cut 30)

about the designers

Ellen Luckett Baker is the author of *1, 2, 3 Sew* and the blogger behind The Long Thread (www.thelongthread.com). Her craft and sewing projects have been featured in numerous publications. Ellen lives in Atlanta with her husband and two daughters.

Amanda Carestio's latest crafting obsessions are mini quilts and furniture makeovers. When she's not bent over her sewing machine or exploring the Blue Ridge Mountains, Amanda enjoys spending quality time with her hubby and super-spoiled canines in Asheville, North Carolina. A member of Lark's Needlearts team, she is the author of *Fa La La La Felt*. Her designs appear in several other Lark books; see more of her creative distractions online at www.digsandbean.blogspot.com.

Savannah Carroll is a self-taught plush artist residing in Chico, California. In May of 2009 she opened up an Etsy shop called Sleepy King (www.etsy.com/shop/sleepyking) and has been sewing full time ever since. Her work has been featured in a New York Gallery, two magazines, and one book, *Craft Challenge: Dozens of Ways to Repurpose Scarves* (Lark 2011). In her free time she enjoys crafting, cooking, thrifting, admiring nature, and playing with her two-year-old son.

Lindy Cline is the creator of PlyTextiles (www.PLYtextiles.com), a brand of items for the modern home. Lindy has been a maker of things from a young age, designing everything from furniture for her dollhouse to handmade jewelry. She has had a long love affair with fabric and fibers. When a favorite sweater accidently shrunk in the wash, Lindy saw raw material for endless projects. At PlyTextiles Lindy loves to put a modern, eco spin on traditional processes for creating warmth in the home.

Karen De Nardi is a designer from Adelaide, Australia, who enjoys making jewelry and ornaments with felt and fabric. Characterized by its delicate style, her work has a good sense of fun and color. Although most of her professional life has involved music, today she is kept busy by the demands of Australian retail outlets and customers around the world. You can see Karen's work at www.denardi.etsy.com.

Catarina Filipe is a Portuguese crafter who has lived among buttons, threads, fabrics, and scissors all her life. Her two step-grandmothers, both seamstresses, taught her to sew at an early age, and she was working on her very own sewing machine by the time she was 8 years old. She is now a full-time crafter, and dreams of seventy-two-hour days so she could have the time to finish all her creative projects. You can take a look at what she's up to on her Facebook page. Just search for Kooka[Licious] and have fun.

Jennifer FitzSimmons is a craft designer who lives in Long Island, New York, where she can usually be found under piles of felt sheets and skeins of yarn. She started her creative endeavors by painting personalized birth announcements. As she continued to experiment with materials and designs, she discovered the beauty of soft, vibrant felt flowers. She now draws on her love of color and texture along with her background in graphic design to create beautiful felt gardens to brighten your home! You can find her wreaths and other designs at www.itz-fitz.com.

Cathy Gaubert is a wife, a momma, and a maker of things. Her days are filled with the antics of three sweet girlies, and the kitchen table is filled with more works-in-progress than you can shake a stick at. Peer into her world at www.handmadecathygaubert.blogspot.com, and do be sure to say hello.

Laura Howard is a self-taught crafter who grew up making things and has never stopped. She lives in Gloucester, England, in a small flat overrun with crafting supplies. Laura works mainly with felt and finds inspiration in its vibrant colors. A love of tea parties, English country gardens, and native British wildlife influences many of her designs. She has been selling her work online since 2007, and writes all about her creative exploits on her blog, www.bugsandfishes.blogspot.com. Laura can be contacted via her website, www.lupinhandmade.com.

Lisa Jordan is an artist who is deeply inspired by nature. Whether she's sewing, felting, or tinkering with vintage buttons, the imprint of nature is evident in the colors, patterns, and textures she chooses. With a nod to sustainability, her work is largely crafted using recycled and natural materials. Reclaimed garment wool is one of her favorite mediums, and one she continues to explore. When she's not creating in her studio, she enjoys gardening, baking, and playing in Minnesota's lakes with her husband and four kids.

Love making the most of your stash? Take a peek at *Stash Happy Patchwork*, the first book in this series, for fresh ideas on using up—and transforming!—your too-lovely-to-toss scraps, impulse yardage buys, and vintage finds.

stash happy FELT

Thom O'Hearn is a former editor for Random House who is now making books at Lark Crafts. When not at work, he is primarily a potter and home brewer, but he occasionally designs bags and totes for friends and family. His store can be found at www.etsy.com/shop/ChanceCeramics.

Mary Rasch has a lifelong passion for creating, whether it is through needle crafting, paper crafting, sculpting, drawing, or painting. Mary, her husband, and her two young children live in Duluth, Minnesota. She sells her projects at a local gift shop and through www.marysmakings.etsy.com. In addition to crafting, Mary enjoys spending time with her family and friends, taking in the beauty of the North Woods, and seeing life through the eyes of her children.

Aimee Ray has been making things from paper, fabric, and clay for as long as she can remember. As a graphic designer in the greeting card and comic book industries, with several personal projects always in the works, she is almost never without something creative in hand, or in mind. Her diverse interests include digital painting and illustration, sewing, and embroidery. She is the author of the best-selling book *Doodle Stitching* as well as *Doodle Stitching: The Motif Collection*. Her designs appear in several Lark publications; see more of her work online at www.dreamfollow.com.

Cynthia Shaffer is a quilter and creative sewer whose love of fabric can be traced back to childhood. At the age of 6, she learned to sew and in no time was designing and sewing clothing for herself and others. After earning a degree in textiles from California State University, Long Beach, Cynthia worked for 10 years as the owner of a company that specialized in the design and manufacture of sportswear. Numerous books and magazines have featured Cynthia's work; she is the author of *Stash Happy Patchwork* (Lark, 2011). She lives with her husband Scott, sons Corry and Cameron, and beloved dogs Harper and Berklee in Southern California. For more information visit her online at www.cynthiashaffer.com or cynthiashaffer.typepad.com.

Cathy Ziegele, motivated by a scandalously naked troll doll, sewed her first felt caveman garment at age six. Her love of sewing grew from there. A retired executive chef, Cathy finds the ease of working with felt to be a nice departure from the chopping and dicing required when working with food. Cathy's pincushions are available for purchase online at www.thedailypincushion.etsy.com, and her digital scrapbooking designs can be found at www.theredporch.com.

index

We'd like to thank the following models: Monica Mouet, Jenny Doh, Dylan Brand, Tiffany Jo Curtis, Ella Furry, and Olivia Furry.